I Love to Tell
the Story

I Love to Tell the Story

the Story

Jeffrey L. Maison

Chalice **Press**
St. Louis, Missouri

Biblical quotations, unless otherwise noted, are from the New Revised Standard Version Bible, copyright 1989, Division of Christian Education of the National Council of Churches of Christ in the USA. Used by permission.

Cover: Kris Vculek

Page design: Elizabeth Wright

This book is printed on acid-free, recycled paper.

Visit Chalice Press on the World Wide Web at
www.chalicepress.com

10 9 8 7 6 5 4 3 2 1   98 99 00 01 02 03

Library of Congress Cataloging–in–Publication Data
Maison, Jeffrey, 1961–
    I love to tell the story: storytelling in children's sermons / by Jeffrey Maison.
        p. cm.
    Includes bibliographical references.
    ISBN 0-8272-1617-3
    1. Children's sermons. 2. Preaching to children. I. Title.
BV4315.M33   1998   97–45699
252'.53—dc21   CIP

Dedicated to
Donna, Bret, and Jordan
without whom I could never have accomplished anything.

Acknowledgments

I will forever be indebted to Dennis Smith and Barbara McBride-Smith. Without Barbara's and Dennis' loving guidance and critique this project would never have been developed. Dennis taught me that careful and thorough biblical exegesis in all preaching and biblical study is not only important but fun. Barbara reminded me of the sheer joy and pleasure that hearing and telling stories brings to children of all ages. To both, my heartfelt thanks and love.

A special thank you to the children and parents of the First Christian Church (Disciples of Christ), Stillwater, Oklahoma. Their love and feedback made this whole project possible.

I would be remiss if I did not thank my wife, Donna, who read, reread, and proofed every word of this book, listened to every story countless times, was my collaborator on the story "Even the Trees Whisper His Name," and is my constant companion and helpmate.

Contents

Introduction

"Where's the Candy?"

Sunday morning, twelve cherub-faced young people sat numb on the chancel steps. The associate pastor was regaling them with an explanation of what the epistles of the New Testament are. One of the young people sat with his back to the associate, another played with his shoes and tugged at his collar. Two of the girls played patty-cake but periodically looked up hopefully at the associate pastor. The whole group of young people fidgeted patiently with hopeful smiles on their faces. As the associate pastor said "Amen" and thanked the young people for coming, several faces looked longingly at the pastor as if to say, "This is it? This can't be the end!" As the young people moved back to their seats, one young girl announced to her mother, "Where's the candy? We didn't get any candy." As she plopped down in the pew, she looked her mother in the face and said, "If we aren't going to get any candy, then why do I have to go down there?"

This event actually occurred, and by mere coincidence it was the very week I began this project. The young girl, although mortifying her mother and father, asked the very question that all ministers should be asking themselves about children's sermons: "Why do we ask the children to come down here?" Why do we have children's sermons, children's moments, or a special message "just for children?" In most cases ministers deliver this sermon because "we have always done it" or "if we do something just for them and then give them paper and crayons, they'll sit quietly through the rest of the service." In either case, the motivation for doing a children's sermon is not for the benefit of the young people whom the ministers are serving but is done solely to benefit themselves and the adult congregants.

I believe this is the reason that most children's sermons are nothing more than three-minute condensed versions of the minister's main sermon. It is what I call the *Reader's Digest* version of the sermon. The same phraseology and terminology are used in the children's sermon as in the main sermon to express and explain complex, abstract, ethical/theological concepts. These words are over the heads of most adults; consequently, they fly over the heads of the children. There is little thought given to the children's sermon, because the minister has already done all the exegetical and manuscript work for the main sermon. It is no small wonder then that the vast majority of children's sermons are "written" early Sunday morning and sometimes just before saying, "Will all the children come up front?"

Ministers are not the only ones who view children's sermons as the "right thing to do" or even as a "necessary evil"; congregational members are just as guilty. I know of no one who has not heard the words "I always get so much more out of the children's sermon than I do out of the regular sermon." There is truth in this statement, mainly because most of us would really prefer to have the condensed version of the sermon without all of the long elaboration. But this statement also points out another truism about the audience of the children's sermon. Ministers are not aiming the message at the children who sit all around them, but they are intentionally entertaining the adult members of the congregation. If you will watch closely and listen intently during children's sermons, you will notice that usually when a loud burst of laughter is heard, it is coming from the congregants, and not one single young person is even smiling.

So where is the candy? That is our job to discern. The Bible is full of stories: tales of love and war, heartbreak and triumph, and ethical guidance. The Bible contains everything that young people need and want to hear and learn about. The trick is finding that golden kernel of truth, that piece of candy, that causes young people to walk away enriched and excited instead of asking, "Where's the candy?" The intent of this introduction is to reflect on how children learn, to clarify why children need and deserve time in every worship service to experience God, and to identify how children's sermons should be constructed to teach and reach today's young people. This leads into the heart of the book: twenty "kid-tested and parent-approved" children's sermons, with exegesis. The sermons are based on the lectionary and include several holiday, special-occasion, and everyday children's sermons.

How Children Learn

Have you ever tried to teach a young person how to play baseball? It is both a rewarding and frustrating experience, much like doing children's sermons. The first thing you notice when you try to teach a young person how to play is that he does not speak your language. She does not understand the technical terminology that we as adults tend to use and take for granted. Children are not little adults and have not developed all the skills that adults have. Can you imagine explaining the fundamental concept of catching a baseball in a glove in these terms?

> Catching a baseball is very easy. This is all you have to do. When the spherical orb makes contact with the synthetic tanned-hide hand-cover, you gently squeeze your opposable thumb toward your four fingers, thus making a closed grasp. Upon inspection of said tanned-hide hand-cover you will discover that the spherical orb is contained therein, and you have caught the ball. Now go out and catch the ball.

Teaching a simple principle such as catching a baseball has now been magnified into a complex undertaking. No parent or coach would ever attempt to teach a young person how to catch in the manner I have outlined, yet we in the church insist that this is the proper way to teach our children the good news of Jesus Christ. Children's sermons are full of complex concepts and words that children do not understand. It is our task as messengers of the good news to learn how children learn and how to use their language without dumbing down the message or talking down to the children.

Piaget's Child Development Theory

The first step in determining how to teach and reach the young people in our congregations is to know who these young people are and how they think. As children grow from infancy to adulthood they progress through a series of cognitive developmental stages. These are best defined by the work of the late Jean Piaget, a Swiss psychologist, whose theories are cited in every major textbook on psychology, education, sociology, and psychiatry.

Piaget divides child development into four periods:"(1) the *sensorimotor* period, 0–2 years; (2) the *preoperational* period, 2–7 years; (3) the period of *concrete operations,* 7–11 years; (4) the period of *formal operations*, 11–15 years."[1] Piaget contends that every child goes through each stage in the same order. There is no skipping of stages; however, the rate of development from one stage to another can and does vary between children. Since most young people who attend children's sermons are between the ages of 2 and 11, sermon givers need to give particular attention to the second and third stages of child development.

The preoperational period sees the child begin to use symbols to represent objects. These symbols include language. "By four years of age the average child in any culture has mastered much of his or her native language. Typically he or she understands and uses a great number of words and uses the main body of the language's grammar effectively."[2]

The child's thinking is *prelogical* or *partly logical* and dominated by perception. In the early stages, the child lacks inductive and deductive logic and cannot understand cause and effect. For example, a child may be able to tell you that nine is greater than eight. But if one were to lay nine pennies end to end in a single-file row and then lay eight additional pennies with a half-inch gap between them in a row parallel to the nine, the judgement of which is greater will be based on perceptions.

oooooooooo

o o o o o o o o

Which of the rows is greater is based on which row is *perceived* to be longer. As the eight pennies spread apart is longer in appearance, the child perceives the greater row to be the row with eight pennies.[3] This is why so many sermon givers only receive blank stares when they ask certain questions. "Do you know what *old* is?" asked a sermon giver. This question was greeted by dead silence. The children had no perception of old and therefore could not answer the question.

Another important characteristic of preoperational thought is what Piaget calls *egocentrism*. "The child thinks that everyone thinks the same way they do, that everyone thinks the same thing they do, and quite logically that everything that they think is right."[4] Children in the preoperational stage have difficulty assuming the viewpoint of others because in their minds there are no other viewpoints than their own.

"Do you know what this is?" asked another sermon giver, holding up a rolled-up piece of paper with a dowel rod at the top and bottom of the paper and red ribbon tied neatly around the roll. "A scroll," announced one young man. "No, it's not a scroll; it's a letter. Like they used to use in Bible times," the sermon giver replied. Both the child and the sermon giver were right. The rolled-up paper looked just like the scrolls the children had made in Sunday school and vacation Bible school—the only reference that the children had to this object. But the sermon giver was also right—the rolled paper represented the letter form of ancient Rome.

By telling the child she was wrong the sermon giver said to the child, "Your thinking is incorrect" and caused the child to spend the entire worship service arguing with her mother that "it was too a scroll." Had the sermon giver reinforced what the child knew and said, "Yes, it is a scroll. And do you know what one of the uses for a scroll was back in Jesus' time? People used to write letters to each other on scrolls," it would have helped to expand the children's knowledge of what a scroll is.

Egocentrism begins slowly to diminish as the child deals with the thoughts of peers that conflict with her own thoughts. However, it should be noted that egocentrism is never eliminated. We all carry a certain degree of egocentrism with us all of our lives.

As children develop and move into the concrete operations period, logic is no longer subordinate to perception in judgment when the child is confronted with concrete problems. When a child is faced with a problem such as the pennies problem, he is able to determine that the row of nine pennies is more than any configuration of eight pennies. As long as the problem she faces is concrete in nature, the child can logically resolve the problem.

Just because children develop the ability to overcome physical perception problems does not mean they are able to apply this technique to non-concrete principles. "The concrete child has difficulties applying his [her] logic to nonconcrete problems. These include complex cerebral problems, hypothetical problems, and problems dealing with the future (which are a type of hypothetical problem). Thus thought is still bound to the concrete and tied to perception."[5]

This is the reason that object-lesson children's sermons must be carefully thought out and prepared in advance. It can be difficult, if not impossible, for children to make the leap from an object's being what it really is to its representing something completely different. Believing that an unopened cookie jar is full of cookies is one thing, but comparing that to believing that the Bible contains the word of God is quite another thing. Children cannot make this shift in logic at this point in their development. "While the concrete operational child may give logically 'correct' answers to the conservation problems, the quality of their reasoning is tied to the concrete aspects of the particular situation."[6]

The age of a child is not necessarily a true indicator of where he is along the developmental strata.[7] The only way to know where each child is, is to get to really know the children in one's congregation. It is just as important for the sermon giver to get to know the children of her church, as it is to get to know the adult congregants, so that meaningful faith-enhancing sermons can be prepared. Children's sermon givers should spend time in the Sunday school classes listening and interacting with the children. Playing games, make believe, and dress-up with a child on her level is the best way to get to know that child and how that child thinks.

Fowler's Faith Development Theory

Before beginning any discussion about how children, or adults for that matter, develop their faith, it is helpful to define faith in some tangible way. The most useful approach I have encountered comes from James Fowler, a theologian and professor of the psychology of religion at Emory University who is considered the leading authority on the theories of faith development. He explains faith as "a person's or group's way of moving into the force field of life. It is our way of finding coherence in and giving meaning to the multiple forces and relations that make up our lives. Faith is a person's way of seeing him- or herself in relation to others against a background of shared meaning and purpose."[8] Faith is something that we are all born with. As Fowler defines it:

> Faith is a universal human concern. Prior to our becoming reli-
> gious or irreligious, before we come to think of ourselves as Catho-
> lics, Protestants, Jews or Muslims, we are already engaged with
> issues of faith. Whether we become nonbelievers, agnostics or
> atheists, we are concerned with how to put our lives together
> and with what will make life worth living. Moreover, we look for
> something to love that loves us, something to value that gives us
> value, something to honor and respect that has the power to sus-
> tain our being.[9]

This definition, although applicable to adults, is particularly helpful when dealing with children. All children look for and need something to love and that will in turn love them. This is the reason that children seek attention and affirmation for what they have done. "Look at this!" is an all-too-familiar statement from children. It is their way of seeking approval, value, honor, respect, and love from those they are with and look up to.

Fowler took the works of Piaget, Lawrence Kohlberg's moral development theories, Erik Erikson's personality development theories, and others, and constructed a six-stage theory of how faith develops. Fowler calls the period up to age three "undifferentiated faith" and considers it a prestage. It is the time when the basic attitudes about trust, courage, hope, and love are formed by the relationship the child has "with the one(s) providing primary love and care."[10] The undifferentiated faith prestage is followed by six stages of faith development: (1) *intuitive-projective faith* (ages 3–6), (2) *mythic-literal faith* (ages 7–11), (3) *synthetic-covential faith* (ages 12–17), (4) *individuative-reflective faith* (ages 18–30), (5) *conjunctive faith* (ages 30–40), (6) *universalizing faith* (after 40).

Since the vast majority of children who attend the children's sermon are between the ages of 3 and 11, it is necessary to understand in detail the intuitive-projective faith stage and the mythic-literal faith stage. "Intuitive-projective faith is the fantasy-filled imitative phase in which the child can be powerfully and permanently influenced by examples, moods, actions, and stories of the visible faith of primally related adults."[11] The child in this stage is greatly influenced by the faith of those adults he or she is most in contact with and respects. As sermon givers, we are in a unique position to influence children's early faith development. The influence is not only in what we say but in how we act out our faith in front of these children. If for no other reason, it becomes critical that the sermon giver spend time with the children they are serving. For just as the pastor is a servant to the congregation's adult members, the children's sermon giver, whether he or she is the pastor or an associate, is a servant to the children. The only effective servant is the one who knows the master's needs, and to know those needs the servant must spend time getting to know the master, the children of the church.

At this stage of faith development children are continually encountering new things for which they have developed no means of knowing or understanding. To deal with these new experiences, children tend to use imagination and stories they have heard to cope "logically" with the new experience. "The imaginative processes underlying fantasy are unrestrained and uninhibited by logical thought. In league with forms of knowing dominated by perception, imagination in this stage is extremely productive of long-lasting images and feelings (positive and negative) that later, more stable and self-reflective valuing and thinking will have to order and sort out."[12] Children at this stage of development are searching for ways to explain and understand the myriad of new and different events and occurrences that they are forced to cope with every day. They may be frightened and confused by what they do not understand or have never encountered before. This is why fairy tales, folk tales, and biblical narratives "provide indirect yet effective ways for children to externalize their inner anxieties and to find ordering images and stories by which to begin to shape their lives."[13]

Bruno Bettelheim, a child therapist, describes a child's need for understanding in this way:

> The child needs ideas on how to bring their house into order, and on that basis be able to create order in his life. The child needs—and this hardly requires emphasis at this moment in our history—a moral education that subtly, and by implication only, conveys to him the advantages of moral behavior, not through abstract ethical concepts but through that which seems tangibly right and therefore meaningful to him.[14]

The use of story will be examined in more detail in the following section, but suffice it to say that children in the intuitive-projective stage need to hear stories to help them sort out the unknown and to help them develop their faith and moral/value systems. Their imagination allows them to move to different places, to see through other's eyes, and to decide whom they wish to be like.[15]

As children age and mature physically, psychologically, and emotionally they also begin to mature in their faith. Between the ages of 7 and 11, some a little earlier and some a little later, children move into the mythic-literal faith stage. The "mythic-literal faith is the stage in which the person begins to take on for him- or herself the stories, beliefs and observances that symbolize belonging to his or her community."[16] It is at this point in their faith development that children begin to understand that who they are as people is directly related to who they associate with; who their community is. And who they are, and who the community is, are tied to the stories and rituals that community shares.

The mythic-literal child is capable of inductive and deductive reasoning. Whereas the intuitive-projective child blends fact and fantasy, the mythic-literal child works hard and effectively to discern the real from the make-believe. These children will begin to demand proof or a demonstration of what you state as fact.[17] Unlike the intuitive-projective child who accepts and expects miracles to happen everyday, for whom a rainbow is a miracle beyond description, the mythic-literal child no longer sees miracles in the everyday. This is why we as sermon givers become frustrated by some of the questions we receive during the children's sermon. We expect the children to be awed by what we have said because it is the "Truth." What we get is a group of children asking "How?" "Why?" and "Can you prove that?" The reality is that some things have to "be taken on faith and cannot be explained," but as sermon givers, we need to give special attention to how "facts" are presented, and whenever "proof" or demonstration can be given, it should be.

The mythic-literal child is moving away from an egocentric persona to being able to take on the perspectives of other people. Because of this otherness "those in stage 2 compose a world based on reciprocal fairness and an immanent justice based on reciprocity."[18] This is an important element of the child's faith development to keep in mind and to use in children's sermons. Many believe that social issues are not appropriate for children's sermons. But children understand fair play and treating others fairly, so why not employ this gift and use it to reinforce the concept that fairness is the way of Christ? This is a golden opportunity for sermon givers to lay a foundation of justice that will stay with the children all of their lives. Social justice should not be ignored, nor should the sermon giver "preach" at the children.

Just as story is important to the development of the intuitive-projective child, story is even more important for the mythic-literal child. "Story becomes the major way of giving unity and value to experience. This is the faith stage of the school child (though we sometimes find the structures dominant in adolescents and in adults)."[19] This stage brings the ability to bind together experiences and give those experiences meaning and expression through the medium of story.

> The convergence of the reversibility of thought with taking the perspective of another combined with an improved grasp of cause-effect relations means that the elements are in place for appropriating and retelling the rich stories one is told. More than this, the elements are in place for youngsters to begin to tell self-generating stories that make it possible to conserve, communicate and compare their experiences and meanings.[20]

Story is the life blood of both the intuitive-projective child and the mythic-literal child. Story helps children develop their sense of being as well as communicate to others who they are. The medium of story has long been overlooked in the church. We are doing a disservice to our children, who depend on story for their faith development, by ignoring the usefulness of story in our church services.

The sermon giver needs to give strict attention to the mythic-literal child's reliance on literalness and reciprocity. If a child is allowed to rely excessively on these two it can result "either in an over controlling, stilted perfectionism or 'works righteousness' or in their opposite, an abasing sense of badness embraced because of mistreatment, neglect or the apparent disfavor of significant others."[21]

As was true with Piaget's theory, Fowler's faith development theory cannot be tied strictly to the age of the child. Each child develops differently and will go through each stage at her or his own developmental pace, reinforcing the necessity for the sermon giver to get to know the children of the congregation.

Up to this point Fowler and I have assumed that the children in our worship services are "church kids," those who have grown up in the church. If this is not the case, the same principles outlined above still apply. However, the age of movement from one stage to another may change. The reality is that children at all the various stages of cognitive and faith development will attend the children's sermon, making it necessary to devise a strategy that will be both effective and meaningful for each and every one of them.

Learning Through Story

Piaget and Fowler have outlined the necessary components that children need in order for them to learn most effectively. But the reality is that in a three- to five-minute children's sermon there is no way to incorporate everything and still have a coherent message that the children will understand. It is then necessary to devise a strategy for effective sermon-giving that will be both meaningful and concise.

The key to effective, meaningful children's sermons is found in both Piaget and Fowler. Piaget and Fowler underlined that the key to learning for all children in the age groups that attend the children's sermon is story. Children in this age group need stories for both their cognitive and spiritual development. Story "can reinforce the imaginative framework of the developing child, give validity to important feelings, promote insights, nourish hope, reduce anxieties, and provide a rich fantasy life."[22] Children in this age group are searching for identity, purpose, and coping mechanisms to make sense of their lives, and story helps children do this.[23]

Children also need moral and ethical instruction. "Children need…a moral education which subtly, and by implication only, conveys to children the advantages of moral behavior, not through abstract ethical concepts but through that which seems tangibly right and therefore meaningful to them."[24] It is through story that children are able to reach out and touch and identify with characters who are faced with moral and ethical decisions. To tell a child about the need for social justice is one thing; it is quite another for a child to hear a story of how a young prince went to live among the poor in his father's kingdom and used all of his money to feed, clothe, and house those who were in need. Gregory Denman explains it this way:

> Stories are lenses through which we view and review all of human experience. No other being on earth can create stories. They have the power to reach deep inside us and command our ardent attention. Through stories we see ourselves. Our individual follies, misgivings, and triumphs. Our personal existence, however trivial it may seem, takes on a cloak of significance.[25]

Story allows children to live vicariously through its characters. Children are able to see how actions can cause pain or joy to others. "Stories provide a 'living through' experience, not just a 'knowing about.' It is in stories that they see played out the facts of their own lives that concern them deeply."[26] They live the experience as if it were their own. "Inside 'story' we can recognize and understand our own motivations, because we are people in the stories, when we enter into 'story' we find the story inside ourselves. 'Story' defines humanity."[27]

Story is the primary learning mode for children who attend children's sermons. It is also through story that children gain ethical and moral understanding. Story can be the bridge between the abstract and real life experiences. It is important to remember that "a fundamental aspect of early Christian preaching was telling stories."[28] And let us not forget that Jesus Christ himself told the most remarkable stories every told—parables. I cannot think of a better spokesperson for the use of story. "Through stories, we see what it is to be alive, to be human."[29]

Hidden Members: Children Deserve Time in Every Service to Experience God

When my family and I moved from Red Oak, Iowa, to Lubbock, Texas, we visited several different churches. One of the churches seemed to be a perfect fit except for one thing: We always felt that they did not want our two young children in worship. After the opening hymn, call to worship, and the children's sermon, people would turn to my wife and me and ask if we were going to send the boys to children's church. "No," we replied, "we always worship as a family." If it had ended there it would have been fine, but one lady in particular was adamant. "Your boys have to go to children's church!" It was the last time we worshiped at that church. Children have a place in our regular Sunday worship and every other worship service conducted by the church.

As a youth minister I am asked one question by older congregants more than any other: "Why can't the young people sit still in worship?" There are two good reasons for this, besides the fact that young people seldom sit still for anything. The first reason is that the adolescents of today's church were never a part of regular Sunday worship while they were growing up. Instead of being in worship where they have the opportunity to learn about worship from adults experiencing meaningful worship, the children went to children's church where they ate cookies, colored pictures, and sang a song or two. Worship is not something in which they participate. The youth of today have unintentionally been socialized to think of worship as something adults do that does not concern them. Children not only need to hear about worship in Sunday school and children's church, but they also need to experience "real adult" worship with adults. Children need to be socialized into the rituals and symbols of our rich Christian heritage.

The second reason for youth and children having difficulty in our worship services is that the services do not address the faith needs of young people. The service is designed by and for adults. Little consideration is given to the spiritual needs of the youth of the church. I do not mean to imply that worship services should be designed only for children and youth. But what I do mean is that worship should have something for all the members, young and old. All worship services should intentionally take into consideration the needs of the whole membership. Children and youth need and deserve time in worship to experience God on their level, and children and youth also need to witness how adults experience God in adult worship in order to continue their spiritual development. A well-constructed, -prepared, and -delivered children's sermon helps meet the spiritual needs of our children and can enhance the worship experience for the adult members. It has long been assumed by adult members that children's growing faith needs are met in Sunday school class. However, spiritual growth is best nurtured when the entire body of Christ worships together.[30]

The Church's Responsibility to Children

Very few people would argue that the church has a responsibility for the development of children's faith. It is about *how* that responsibility should be carried out that arguments develop. There are many approaches to this problem, but the key to remember is that whatever we do we should not put impediments in the way of our children's growth. "The church's ministry with children should do nothing that would block future reasoning about faith. Rather, it should provide conditions that enhance the possibility of growth in faithful thinking and reasoning."[31] When we deny our children access to the communal worship setting, we are setting road blocks. Instead of enhancing their possibility of growth we are inadvertently stunting their faith development.

During one children's sermon I took the children on a treasure hunt. We had a map that contained several clues that would lead us to the "buried treasure," the Bible. The first clue asked the children to "go sixteen paces to the place where everybody eats when they come to church." I admit that I made several cognitive mistakes in the way I phrased the question that made it impossible for the children to respond in the way I wanted them to. However, even after I rephrased the directive to "go sixteen paces to the place where the communion bread and cups are" the children did not know where to go. I must admit that this is a perfect example of a poorly prepared and constructed children's sermon, but I still found it shocking that children born and raised in the Disciples of

Christ church did not know where the Lord's table was. Part of the reason was because these children are never in the worship service during communion. Instead of being in worship learning about the importance of the sacrament from adults actively participating in the rituals of the church, they are in children's church hearing about the rituals of the church. By taking our children out of the worshiping community we have blocked their growing faith and understanding of who they are within the body of Christ.

In most churches, shortly after an infant is born, she is brought before the worshiping community and is either baptized or dedicated into the body of Christ. Included in the service of baptism or dedication is a charge to the church to raise, nurture, and care for the spiritual growth of the infant. When we deny children access to worship we are in direct contradiction to the pledge we have made to God, and to ourselves, to nurture the child's growth in the faith. Adults in the church must ask themselves, "How do we as adults carry out the promises made at the baptism or dedication service?"[32] The act of baptism, in particular, as well as the act of dedication, recognizes that a person is a full member of the body of Christ. They are not part-time members, but whole and complete members who must be accorded the same rights, privileges, and limitations as all other members of the body. As a member of the body of Christ each child "has a meaningful place in what that family does as a group, including worship....Children should be involved in worship with adults because the church follows Jesus Christ, assumes responsibility for children at their dedication or baptism, and is designed as a covenant community."[33] It is impossible to be both "in Christ" and "out of Christ" at the same time, yet this is the attitude that many hold when it comes to children in worship.

"It is within the community of the body of Christ, the church, that persons come to experience the essential inclusiveness of a shared calling to faith by God through Christ."[34] Worship is the most symbolic and effective act of the body of Christ. It is in the communal sharing of scripture, sermon, prayer, praise, song, and communion "that the cognitive elements of faith are joined with its confessional, interior, and affective elements."[35] If children are excluded from the most visible communal aspect of the body of Christ, they will not learn the importance, joy, and bonding that can only occur in worship when the whole of the body gathers to celebrate God's grace and love. Worship is not solely for the purpose of praising God; it is also for the building up of the community. Fellowship and the unity of community are forged in the bonds of worship. Children learn that they are a part of something much bigger than themselves and their immediate family when they are able to worship as the whole community.

The key element of worship is response, the community's "celebrative response to what God has done, is doing, and promises to do."[36] If children are kept from the community, they are not only being blocked from learning *how* to express their own response to God, but also from actually *being able* to respond to God. However, "when children participate joyously with other members of the congregation, they experience a sense of 'belonging' that feeds their work of faith development."[37] When children are excluded from the worship setting we are sending a clear message to them that they are not a "real" part of the faith community. Children at a very young age understand the importance their parents put on attending worship. Children may not understand why worship is important to the parents, but they do know that it is important. Otherwise why would adults attend worship regularly? Children grow in their faith development when they are able fully to participate in the same important activity that their parents do. As the mature parts of the body we have a responsibility not only to supply the tools necessary for faith development, such as knowledge of scripture that is taught in Sunday school, but also to include children in the very activity of faith response: worship.

Many churches provide children a separate children's worship-time that runs concurrently with the adult worship service. I will not argue that if adequate time and energy is devoted to this activity it can offer opportunities for worship that are appropriate to the children's level of development. I also will not argue that these children's worship-times might also provide some parents the opportunity to participate more completely in the adult worship experience. However, "a separate children's church-time divides the family—and the congregation—as a worshiping group."[38] The separate children's worship-time also reinforces in the mind of children that they are not really a part of the whole body of Christ. Children are sent away, with the best of intentions, at the very moment when the adult members state they are gathered "in Christ" as the unified body of Christ. Including children in worship helps "children develop a sense of belonging to the faith community, acquaints them with the traditions and rituals of the church, and introduces them to the minister and other adult members of the church. At the same time, the presence of children would add to the wholeness of the worship experience for adults."[39] Children need to be intentionally included in the total life of the church, not just for their own faith development, but for the faith development of every member of the faith community. As Paul reminds us, "If one member suffers, all suffer together with it" (1 Corinthians 12:26).

Children Want to Worship

Children not only need to experience worship in order to learn and express their growing faith; children also want to worship. "Children are ready to worship. They are ready to acknowledge, rehearse, and proclaim with the gathered community."[40] This statement may seem hard to believe, but it only takes a little observation to realize that children are involved in the act of worship all the time. "Children worship with each new discovery of their lives: stars, puppies, and even snowflakes. Reverence, respect, love, awe, praise, adoration, appreciation, and honor come naturally to children."[41]

One year I decided that even our youngest school-age children would want to participate in a special church offering that went to overseas missions. I went from Sunday school class to Sunday school class giving each child a small cardboard "blessing box" and explained to each class what the offering was for and how they could help. Before I left each class, I asked them to remember to bring their boxes back next week so we could bless their special offering. I was not expecting a high return of boxes and certainly did not expect to collect much money, but I believed that I was planting a seed that would blossom later in life.

The next Sunday I was amazed and delighted to discover that of the forty-five blessing boxes I distributed, forty-one were returned with money. What one first grader did that Sunday morning I will remember for the rest of my life. Most of the boxes were filled with dollar bills supplied by the children's parents, but this child, with a smile from ear to ear across her angelic face, had a box filled with pennies, nickels, a few dimes, and several quarters.

I asked the children to place their blessing boxes on a special altar we had constructed for the offering. When it was her turn to place her box on the altar she walked very slowly and held her box out away from her, with her eyes locked on the floor. With great care she placed her box on the top of the altar, stopped, and with a smile, looked to the sky and then hurried back to the rest of the children. After the worship service her dad came up to me and said: "You know, that was her entire life savings. Last Sunday when we got home she went right into her room and emptied her entire piggy bank into the box. She wouldn't even let me or her mother give her any money for the offering." Children may not understand all of the intricate details of worship, but they do have a need to respond to God, and in some ways they are more capable of demonstrating their response than we adults are.

The major argument against including children in worship is that they "do not get anything out of worship." If one means "Does a child get anything out of worship in terms of Piaget's cognitive development theories?" then the answer is no. But then again, the answer is also applicable to the average adult sitting in the pew on Sunday morning. What children do get out of being in worship is the sense of belonging to the body of Christ. When children are not only included in worship but are truly welcome in worship, they know they are part of the whole community. Nevertheless, there is a very real danger in trying to qualitatively measure "what children get out of worship." When part of the body attempts to measure what another part of the body is getting out of worship it causes divisions that lead to the whole body no longer worshiping. Unless we are ready to measure each and every person's worship experience to make sure that they have "got enough out of it," it is unfair to hold children to this kind of worship experience criterion.

On a cognitive level, when children are included in worship they are learning about worship, what it is, and how it is done. Through the simple act of observation children begin to internalize how their particular faith community worships. They are able to observe when to sit, when to stand, when to sing, when to speak, and when to share feelings of joy and sorrow. Bit by bit the pieces of the worship puzzle begin to take form for children when they are able to participate fully in the activity of response.

It is true that children need to participate in worship to learn the cognitive rules and forms of worship, but on a spiritual level children are already able to "know, love, and worship God in ways that are appropriate for their development and understanding....Children are not just *learning* about God through explanation and interpretation, but children are *worshiping* through entering into the experience of the presence of God. The children are participating and 'taking in' the experience."[42] Children can and do respond to God in our worship services. Their responses may not be the same as adults', but this does not mean that their responses are any less valid. Children will experience awe and wonder in worship as well as boredom and confusion. The reward and the value of having children intimately involved in the worship experience is when they experience those moments of awe and wonder in the presence of God in the midst of the worshiping community. When we deny children access to the worship experience we are preventing them from experiencing and responding to the awe and wonder of God that is only found when the whole body of Christ proclaims the gospel together.

Children construct faith meanings from the totality of their experiences. Everything they do, everything they see, and everything they hear shapes their understanding and development of faith. Whereas adults separate scripture readings from prayer and rituals, children do not. For children there is no separation between the Bible, church traditions, and belief, nor do they separate knowledge from their own feelings and "the actions they observe in others or that they themselves initiate. Rather, they approach life as a whole."[43] Faith is not a group of unrelated activities from which an individual can pick and choose. Faith is a single, unified event that has many facets. Children are unable, and rightly so, to distinguish between the activities and the event. So if children are to fully develop their faith, they need to experience the whole of Sunday morning. They need the experience of Sunday school, the experience of fellowship between Sunday school and worship, and the experience of coming together with the entire body of Christ to worship God.

Finally, it should be remembered that Jesus set the example for the inclusion of children in worship. When the disciples attempted to send the children away who had only come so that "he might touch them," Jesus became angry. He was angry with the adults who were denying the children the ability to worship. Today, more than ever, the words of Jesus need to be remembered and lived again in our churches: "Let the little children come to me; do not stop them; for it is to such as these that the kingdom of God belongs" (Mark 10:14).

Telling the Story

Teaching and including children in the traditions and the life work of the church is not an easy task. The strategies we employ must be carefully planned, thought out, presented, and evaluated just as all parts of worship are carefully planned for adults. But if we take our cue from Jesus and the gospel writers we will discover that the answer is found in the art of storytelling. That reminds me of a story...

The master taught in parables and stories, which his disciples listened to with great joy—and occasionally with frustration, for they wanted something much deeper. The master refused to change his teaching style. To all their objections he would say, "You still do not understand that the shortest distance between a human being and Truth is a story."[44]

The heart of this book consists of twenty children's sermons that illustrate how the techniques outlined in the introduction can be applied to create messages that matter and mean something to the audience they are intended for. I have included a variety of lectionary biblical texts—from holiday to regular Sunday worship—to demonstrate that even the most difficult text can be used, and a message that young children can understand can be achieved, if the children's sermon giver is willing to put in the time and effort. The order follows the sequence of Sundays in the church year from the first Sunday in Advent through the Sundays after Pentecost, with an intermingling of the three years of the lectionary cycle.

Each children's sermon includes the biblical text and a brief exegetical analysis of the main point or a key point of the text. A children's sermon story is presented that points to the main or key point of the biblical text. Finally, a brief hermeneutical proposal is presented in support of the selected story. It should be noted that these stories can be used just as they are, but a story must speak directly to the storyteller. It should also be remembered that once you have found the "perfect" story for a biblical text, you will find a still more "perfect" story later. It will seem as if you always find the "perfect" story the day after you needed it. Just remember there is always a better story out there somewhere. Save them and use them.

Good Exegesis Is Critical

The noted professor of homiletics Dr. Fred Craddock says, "The most important single contributing factor to consistently effective preaching is study and careful preparation."[45] Although this is true for the adult sermon, it is critical for the children's sermon. All too often children's sermons are written late Saturday night or Sunday morning, with little or no thought given to them. Because of this lack of study and preparation, the point of the scripture text tends to become lost on the children, and the children's sermon becomes meaningless.

The beginning point of any good children's sermon is the sermon giver's own study of the scripture. "Let the Word itself speak to you. A message for children does not start with an object looking for a truth; it is a truth looking for a way to be proclaimed, understood, and used."[46] Good exegesis is a must if we are truly attempting to proclaim the good news. It is not as important that we convey the exact biblical text to our children, as that we should convey the message of the biblical text. The stories that I have selected do not necessarily parallel the biblical text, and in some cases, the biblical text cannot even be guessed at from the stories themselves. But in all cases the message, meaning, or moral imperative of the biblical text is clearly evident. The only way to find a story that helps our children find the message of the text is through careful, systematic exegesis. As Sara Covin Juengst says, "Do exegesis on the text; let its real meaning surface."[47]

Part of the difficulty for most sermon givers is the "three-point sermon" training they received in seminary. This sermon model contends that every effective sermon should have three points. However, this model does not work well with children, as I have noted above (see Piaget's cognitive development theory). Our job as children's sermon givers is to find a single point or golden kernel of truth to lift up. This is not to say that some texts will not have several points, because many will. "However, thorough exegesis of the passage in its context may reveal that all those ideas are really subordinate to and supportive of a larger overarching issue."[48] At other times the lectionary texts are just too much for children to handle in one sitting. These passages need to be pared down to workable units. But the only way to know if the text is too large or if it contains two or more discernable pericopes is through careful and thorough study and preparation.

Finally, in preparing for the sermon it is important to know your audience. As stated above, it is critical to know where on the developmental scale your children are. However, in a normal children's sermon setting you will have a wide variety of children at different levels, and you must decide where to aim your stories. I believe that it is best to shoot high and aim for the highest developmental level in the group. This is what I have done with all of the stories presented here. Children from seven to eleven will get much from each story, whereas those who are younger may only catch a bit of it. But because they are stories, and stories are critical to the development of children, the younger children will still benefit from them. However, if you only have children who are four and five years old participating in the children's sermon, then I would encourage you to seek out stories more age-appropriate for them.

Preparation for Storytelling

While preparing and presenting these children's sermons to my own congregation, I stumbled across several bits of information that I hope will make the presentation of this type of children's sermon more fulfilling and enriching for children. The first, and in many ways the most important, lesson I learned was the need to focus the children's attention and prepare them for a time of listening. Simply asking the children to come forward and waiting for them to sit down on the chancel steps does not "tell" them it is time to listen. Children need clear and understandable signals as to what is expected of them and when. Until they are made aware that this is a special time of listening they will, and do, feel free to talk, walk, and play. This is what happened to me. To make this a special time of listening I began to remain standing until all the children were gathered. Then I asked them to stand in a circle and hold hands. We stood in our circle holding hands until everyone was ready to listen. Once we were all ready, together we sat down on the floor, maintaining our circle. This worked well, and after just a few weeks of instruction the children began to gather in the circle, holding hands without a word of instruction. This worked well for me and fits who I am. The point is, before you can speak, you have to have listeners prepared to hear.

As a minister, the second lesson in preparation and presentation was the hardest for me to learn. Scripture is the basis of each children's sermon and story. The stories certainly stand on their own and are useful tools for teaching important life lessons. However, the point of using the stories is to help young children understand the Sunday lectionary text. With this in mind, it seemed only natural to read the entire scripture text to the children and then tell a story. The harsh reality is that I lost the children's attention, and no matter how good the story was or how well told, I could not get them to refocus. If you are using the same scripture text that is being used for the adult sermon, the text does not need to be read twice. Instead, several other options can be used, depending on the text and the story being used. One can read a single verse or key phrase from the text that encapsulates the point of the scripture. This brings the Bible in without losing the attention of the children. Another way that works well is to say something like, "The preacher is going to read to us in a few minutes a Bible story about…and it reminded me of a story." This not only provides you with a nice entry into the story; it also helps prepare the children to listen to the scripture reading and adult sermon. Another option is to say something like, "I was reading the scripture that the preacher will read in a few minutes and it made me think of a question….That question made me think of a story." This is particularly effective for stories that may not seem to have a surface connection to the text. By stating the question, you have planted the seed for what you want the children to listen for.

It is also important to tell the children the cultural background of each story. Telling children that a story comes from the Sonike people of Africa or is a Native Alaskan folktale helps children to grow in tolerance and understanding of the different cultures in the world. Knowing where a story comes from also helps children to form mental pictures in their heads. Knowing a story is from Alaska, children immediately begin to picture snow and ice, igloos and polar bears. Cultural awareness among the children also gives the sermon giver the opportunity to explain difficult or troublesome customs and new words and phrases. It is important, however, to be precise and accurate with your cultural identification. A Chinese, Korean, or Vietnamese story should be indentified as such. But when the origin of a story is unclear as to the specific culture, you should use the geographic regional name, such as Middle Eastern, Asian, or South American. Native American and Native Alaskan stories should be discribed by their tribal origin: Iroquois, Ogallah, or Poncan. By taking the time to properly identify the culture of each story we are teaching a small lesson in tolerance and reconciliation.

You need to find ways to involve the children actively in the story, bring them into the story world itself. Simple hand motions that they can do at certain times during the telling of the story can be helpful. For example, in "Czar Trojan's Ears" the czar has the ears of a goat. I asked the children, "What do goat ears look like?" The children and I immediately put our hands to the sides of our heads with the fingers pointing up. I then asked, "What does a goat sound like?" "Naaaa," was the universal reply. "In this story," I continued, "every time you hear the words the 'ears of a goat,' put on your ears and make a goat sound." Throughout this complex story the children were focused and listened intently so they would not miss a single "ears of a goat." Another participation tool I discovered was to have the children tell part of the story. In "The Tinker King" the king always asks his questions three times. I asked the children to say the king's question while I told the other character's answers to the question. Not every story lends itself to group participation, nor should it be used every time. But when it is used appropriately it can be a wonderful experience.

The final lesson I learned about the preparation and presentation of children's sermons is where to locate quality stories. Many wonderful hours were spent sitting on the floor of the Stillwater Oklahoma Public Library reading folktales. Public libraries are treasure troves waiting to be discovered by ministers. Hundreds of stories are there sitting on the shelves begging to be used. Instead of being a chore, my visits to the library became a weekly pilgrimage to discover new and different stories. Every good story was checked out and added to my growing file of stories. The most important and rewarding lesson I learned from this whole project happened while sitting in front of the children's folktale section. Not all stories can be done orally; some are best when read individually. Therefore, I began to not only sit on the floor, but to read the stories out loud so I could hear them as well. It was not long before I would have a small audience of children gathered around listening to the stories I was reading. In a very unintentional and most unexpected way I was able to share my love of stories with strangers.

NOTES

[1] Barry J. Wadsworth, *Piaget for the Classroom Teacher* (New York: Longman Publishing, 1978), p. 12.

[2] Ibid., p. 16.

[3] Ibid., p. 16f.

[4] Ibid., p. 19.

[5] Ibid.

[6] Ibid., p. 20.

[7] Ibid., p. 12; and Sara Covin Juengst, *Sharing Faith with Children: Rethinking the Children's Sermon* (Louisville: Westminster/John Knox Press, 1994), p. 30.

[8] James W. Fowler, *Stages of Faith: The Psychology of Human Development and the Quest for Meaning* (San Francisco: Harper and Row, 1981), p. 4.

[9] Ibid., p. 5.

[10] Ibid., p. 121.

[11] Ibid., p. 133.

[12] Ibid.

[13] Ibid., p. 130.

[14] Bruno Bettelheim, *The Uses of Enchantment: The Meaning and Importance of Fairy Tales* (New York: Alfred A. Knopf Inc., 1976), p. 5.

[15] Fowler, *Stages of Faith*, p. 134, and Juengst, *Sharing Faith With Children*, p. 87.

[16] Fowler, *Stages of Faith*, p. 149.

[17] Ibid., p. 135f.

[18] Ibid., p. 149.

[19] Ibid.

[20] Ibid., p. 136.

[21] Ibid., p. 150.

[22] Bob Barton and David Booth, *Stories in the Classroom: Storytelling, Reading Aloud and Roleplaying with Children* (Portsmouth, New Hampshire: Heinemann, 1990), p. 13.

[23] Bettelheim, *The Uses of Enchantment*, p. 309.

[24] Ibid., p. 5.

[25] Gregory A. Denman, *Sit Tight, and I'll Swing You a Tail: Using and Writing Stories with Young People* (Portsmouth, New Hampshire: Heinemann, 1991), p. 4.

[26] Barton and Booth, *Stories in the Classroom*, p. 12.

[27] Norma J. Livo and Sandra A. Rietz, *Storytelling: Process and Practice* (Littleton, Colorado: Libraries Unlimited, Inc., 1986), p. 4.

[28] David L. Barr, *New Testament Story: An Introduction* (Belmont, California: Wadsworth Publishing, 1987), p. 20.

[29] Denman, *Sit Tight, and I'll Swing You a Tail*, p. 4.

[30] Dorothy Jean Furnish, "Rethinking Children's Ministry," in *Rethinking Christian Education: Explorations in Theory and Practice*, ed. David S. Schuller (St. Louis: Chalice Press, 1993), p. 81.

[31] Ibid., p. 74.

[32] Elizabeth J. Sandell, *Including Children in Worship: A Planning Guide for Congregations* (Minneapolis: Augsburg Publishing, 1991), p. 7.

[33] Ibid.

[34] W. Alan Smith, *Children Belong in Worship: A Guide to the Children's Sermon* (St. Louis: CBP Press, 1984), p. 35.

[35] Ibid.

[36] John E. Burkhart, *Worship* (Philadelphia: Westminster Press, 1982), p. 17.

[37] Furnish, "Rethinking Children's Ministry," p. 78.

[38] Sandell, *Including Children in Worship*, p. 7.

[39] Furnish, "Rethinking Children's Ministry," p. 82; also see Sandell, *Including Children in Worship*, p. 12.

[40] Juengst, *Sharing Faith with Children*, p. 19.

[41] Sandell, *Including Children in Worship*, p. 15.

[42] Ibid.

[43] Furnish, "Rethinking Children's Ministry," p. 82.

[44] A Jewish folktale.

[45] Fred B. Craddock, *As One Without Authority: Essays on Inductive Preaching* (Enid, Oklahoma: The Phillips University Press, 1974), p. 98.

[46] Juengst, *Sharing Faith with Children*, p. 101.

[47] Ibid.

[48] Craddock, *As One Without Authority*, p. 103.

1

The Wise Master

Mark 13:32–37   **Week 1 of Advent, Year A**

But about that day or hour no one knows, neither the angels in heaven, nor the Son, but only the Father. Beware, keep alert; for you do not know when the time will come. It is like a man going on a journey, when he leaves home and puts his slaves in charge, each with his work, and commands the doorkeeper to be on the watch. Therefore, keep awake—for you do not know when the master of the house will come, in the evening, or at midnight, or at cockcrow, or at dawn, or else he may find you asleep when he comes suddenly. And what I say to you I say to all: Keep awake.

Comments on the Text

It is reassuring to know that concern for what will happen at the end of time is nothing new. What happens when we die, how will the end of the world occur, who will be saved, and who will be condemned are questions that humanity has asked, worried over, and fretted about from the beginning of time. Even those most devoted followers of Jesus: Peter, James, John, and Andrew (13:3), the ones who knew him most intimately, wondered and worried about the end times. Mark 13, referred to as the "Little Apocalypse" (or "Synoptic Apocalypse," cf. Matthew 24; Luke 21), is a text addressing these age-old questions.[1]

The parable "A Man Going on a Journey,"[2] offers Christians not only hope for the future, but hope to live in the present. Before beginning an in-depth analysis of the text it may be important to remember who Mark addressed in this gospel story and what their "present" socio-political conditions were. Verses 9–13 are not a forecast of future persecutions, although future persecution has and, in some cases, still occurs, but are a presentation of current events. The beatings, the trials, the betrayals, and the deaths "are precisely what the first readers of Mark were experiencing in their missionary preaching to the Gentiles."[3] Thus, the parable becomes instructive as well as empowering. It empowers the readers for the trouble that is, and for the trouble that is to come.

It is also important to remember the socio-political and economic roles of the characters in "A Man Going on a Journey." Masters and servants "represent a major way that society organized itself."[4] The roles of master and servant are well defined. The most striking connection between the two is the solidarity that exists between the master and servant. It is a bond that transcends the legal requirements. By twentieth century North American standards this connectedness is hard to understand. We live in an era regulated by law, but in the master-servant societies of antiquity, the inequality is regulated and legitimated by custom more than law. "Those servants who feel themselves aggrieved...have no appeal within the legal system. They can act only outside it."[5] Because of this unequal system, servants choose to accept the protection of a master in exchange for giving up control of themselves. Not only is every facet of life controlled by the master, but the master also exerts control from afar. Galilee two thousand years ago "was characterized by absentee landlords and a mixed population in which the indigenous people were at the bottom of the social hierarchy."[6] The absentee landlord figures prominently in this and other parables of Jesus, and was widely used by others as well as a metaphor for God's relationship with Israel.

Chapter 13 is Jesus' farewell to the disciples, functioning like John 14–17, the great commission in Matthew 28:16–20, and the resurrection appearance in Jerusalem in Luke 24:36–49. In each of the Gospel accounts the disciples are commissioned to act. In John the command is "to be united in love with Christ and with one another," in both Luke and Matthew the command is to "engage in the mission to the Gentiles," but in Mark the command is to "watch for the coming of the Son of man."[7] It is important to note that the command to watch does not nullify the other two commands, and, as we will see, the command to watch actually reinforces the commands to love and to do mission work.

During the season of Advent the command to watch is of central importance. Advent is a time of watchful, hopeful anticipation. "A man going on a journey," (13:34) tells the reader that the servants are very aware of the absence of their master. Because the master is their protector, there is a sense of longing and anxious anticipation for the master's return by the servants. The wait may be long and anxious, but it is also expected. The command to "be on the watch" (13:34), reminds the reader that the return of the master is certain; when the master will return, however, is a mystery.

However, the command to "watch" is not a directive to sit idly by doing nothing while waiting for the master to return. It is instead a directive to "work" diligently at the tasks over which each has been put "in charge" (13:34) while awaiting the expected return. As Pheme Perkins notes: "The servants know the tasks that have been entrusted to them, but do not know when the master will return. The only way to be certain of the master's praise is to be faithful to the tasks assigned. Faithful servants do not need to know when the master will return."[8] Waiting and watching is a proactive event or could be considered a test. The master's departure provides a test for the servants. In this way the master will know the fidelity of the servants. It also provides a metaphorical framework for understanding Jesus' proclamation of the kingdom as both present and absent.[9]

The text does not provide an answer to when, how, or where the end time will come for, "only the Father" knows (13:32). But the text does provide hope for a certain, yet unknown future, as well as how to live in the "in-between time." Followers are fully "in charge" (13:34) of this world during the master's absence. Yet, at the same time the servants have been charged with specific instructions for how to operate the "home" (13:34). "This Gospel addresses disciples as those who are bereft of their master, fully in charge here, and responsible to be ready at any moment to give account of their stewardship when the master returns."[10] Therefore, "what I say to you I say to all: Keep awake" (13:37).

CHILDREN'S SERMON ━━━━━━━━━━━━━━━

The Wise Master

There once was a wise master teacher who lived with a great number of students in a run-down temple. The students supported themselves by begging for food in the busy streets of a nearby town.

Many of the students complained about their humble living conditions. So one day the old master said to his students, "We must repair the walls of our temple. But, since we spend our days studying and meditating, there is no time to earn the money we need for the repairs. Therefore, I have thought of a simple solution."

All the students eagerly gathered closer to hear the words of their teacher. "Each of you must go into the town and steal goods that can be sold for money," said the master. "Then we will be able to do the good work of repairing our temple."

The students were stunned at this suggestion. "Why would the wise master ask us to do something so dishonest?" thought the students. But because they respected the master greatly, they assumed he must have good judgement and did not protest.

The wise master sternly warned them, "In order not to destroy our reputation by committing an illegal and immoral act, be certain to steal only when no one is looking. I do not want anyone to be caught."

When the master walked away, the students discussed the plan among themselves.

"It is wrong to steal," said one. Another asked, "Why has our wise master asked us to do this?"

Yet another retorted, "It will allow us to rebuild our temple to its former glory, which is a good thing."

Finally, the students agreed that their teacher was wise and just and surely must have a sensible reason for making such an unusual request. And so they set out eagerly for the town, promising each other that they would not disgrace their school by being seen and getting caught stealing. "Be careful," they called to one another. "Do not let anyone see you stealing."

Well, that is, all the students except one young boy who sat quietly on the steps of the temple. The wise master saw the boy sitting on the steps so sadly that he asked, "Why are you so sad, my boy? Hurry before you are left behind by the others."

The boy looked up at the master with tears in his eyes and said, "I cannot follow your instructions to steal where no one will see me, master. Wherever I go, I am always there watching. My own eyes will see me steal."

The wise master tearfully embraced the boy. "I was just testing the integrity of my students," he said. "And you are the only one who has passed the test!"[11]

Reflections on the Story

In searching for a story for this text it would be easy to seek out a story of impending doom and destruction. However, the reason the disciples asked about what will happen in the end times was not their anticipation of doom and destruction, but because they were seeking a better place and time. Therefore, a story must contain a search or a desire for a better place than what the characters currently have. A story for this text must also have the element of control. A "master" who has the power to exert control over what the "servants" do. The "master" must also expect the servants to faithfully complete the tasks assigned. The story should also contain the notion of watching.

The "Wise Master" offers a story of disciples (students) desiring a better place, the repair of their run-down temple. The master of the temple has control over his students. Here in the story of "The Wise Master" we have a student who knows what his "work" is, honesty and doing what is right, and is faithful to his work. Just as the master's departure is considered a test in Mark, the master in the story tests his students. Only the student who is "watching" passes the test. "The Wise Master" reminds us all to "keep awake" and do as we have been "charged."

Alternative Children's Sermon

This story may present a moral dilemma. What will the children's reaction be to an adult authority figure (the wise master) who tells his students to go out and steal? Stealing is certainly not a message that we want to encourage in the church, and there is some danger that this message could be heard by some children in the audience. However, when I presented this story to the children of my own church, almost all of them said one of the messages was "Don't steal." "The Wise Master" expresses the meaning of the text extremely well, but because of the possible mixed message it could give, I offer "The Burning of the Rice Fields" as an alternative story that can be used with Mark 13:32–37.

ALTERNATIVE CHILDREN'S SERMON ━━━━━━━━━━━━━━

The Burning of the Rice Fields

L ong ago in Japan there was a small village. To the east of the village was the great ocean; to the west was a high mountain. Some of the men made their living by fishing, but all the other villagers—men, women, and children—worked every day in the rice fields that lay on top of the mountain. Every morning the villagers climbed the mountain path to work the fields. And every evening they trudged home to sleep in their huts. Everyone, that is, except grandfather, and his grandson, Ti, who lived on the mountain. It was grandfather's job to keep the fires lit at night to keep the wild animals out of the rice.

It happened very early one morning, just when the rice fields had turned gold and dry, perfect for harvesting. The villagers had just begun to move about, doing their morning chores before they started their trek to the top of the mountain. That morning, as was grandfather's custom, he went to the edge of the mountain to watch the sun rise. However, this morning he could not see the rising sun. But what he saw brought fear to his soul.

Quickly he ran to their hut where Ti was sleeping. "Ti, get up," shouted grandfather.

"Oh, grandfather, let me sleep," complained a sleepy Ti.

"Do as I say," the old man shouted. "Grab a burning stick from the fire and follow me."

This time Ti obeyed, for he had never heard grandfather sound so urgent. So, without understanding why, Ti got out of bed, grabbed a burning stick from the fire, and ran out to join grandfather, who was thrusting his burning stick into the dry rice. Grandfather spat out a command: "Burn the rice fields."

"But, grandfather, this is our village's food," protested Ti. "Without it we will all go hungry!"

"Do as I do," grandfather shouted over his shoulder.

With tears streaming down his face, Ti took his burning stick and began to set the precious rice fields on fire. Soon smoke from the rice fields billowed up, filling the sky.

Down below a priest saw the smoke and began to ring the bells to alert the people. Soon every man, woman, and child was running up the steep mountain path as quickly as they could. When they finally reached the top of the mountain all they could see were flames consuming their precious rice. Every last grain was destroyed.

"Who set the fire?" the people cried.

Grandfather stepped forward and said, "I did it."

"You, grandfather? But why?"

"Look," grandfather said, pointing out to sea. What they saw was a gigantic tidal wave almost as high as the mountain they stood on rushing toward the village below. When the wave reached the village it crushed the houses like a giant hand smashing paper cups. Then a second wave and a third followed, until the whole village was under tons of water. The villagers looked at their ruined homes and their burnt fields in despair.

"We have nothing left," one voiced cried.

"On the contrary," said an old woman. "We have our lives. Everyone has survived."

"This afternoon we will start all over," the village elder said. "But first, we must thank grandfather for his act of courage and wisdom. His quick action saved our people."

All of the people agreed. And for the rest of his life the village honored grandfather for his courage and wisdom.[12]

Reflections on the Alternative Story

"The Burning of the Rice Fields" is not the perfect fit like that of "The Wise Master," but it does bring home the point of the Mark scripture text. In this story the grandfather is the faithful servant who not only "keeps awake" watching over the field but dutifully performs the job that he has been assigned. When the village is threatened by the tidal wave, the grandfather does the only thing that he can do to faithfully perform his duty to take care of his fellow villagers: He burns the fields to alert them to the danger and thus moves them to safety. "The Burning of the Rice Fields" story reminds us to stay vigilant, to "keep awake," and to do as we have been "charged."

NOTES

[1] Lamar Williamson, Jr., *Mark* (Louisville: John Knox Press, 1983), p. 236.

[2] I have chosen to use the title given to this parable by Bernard Brandon Scott in *Hear Then the Parable: A Commentary on the Parables of Jesus* (Minneapolis: Fortress Press, 1989), p. 4.

[3] Williamson, *Mark*, p. 238.

[4] Scott, *Hear Then the Parable*, p. 205.

[5] Ibid., p. 206.

[6] Ibid., p. 207.

[7] Williamson, *Mark*, p. 238.

[8] Pheme Perkins, "The Gospel of Mark," in *The New Interpreter's Bible*, vol. 8 (Nashville: Abingdon Press, 1995), p. 694.

[9] Scott, *Hear Then the Parable*, p. 213.

[10] Williamson, *Mark*, p. 240.

[11] A Japanese folktale.

[12] A Japanese folktale.

2

The Tinker King

Isaiah 61:1–4, 10–11   **Week 3 of Advent, Year A**

The spirit of the Lord GOD is upon me, because the LORD has anointed me; he has sent me to bring good news to the oppressed, to bind up the brokenhearted, to proclaim liberty to the captives, and release to the prisoners; to proclaim the year of the LORD's favor, and the day of vengeance of our God; to comfort all who mourn; to provide for those who mourn in Zion—to give them a garland instead of ashes, the oil of gladness instead of mourning, the mantle of praise instead of a faint spirit. They will be called oaks of righteousness, the planting of the LORD, to display his glory. They shall build up the ancient ruins, they shall raise up the former devastations; they shall repair the ruined cities, the devastations of many generations.

I will greatly rejoice in the LORD, my whole being shall exult in my God; for he has clothed me with the garments of salvation, he has covered me with the robe of righteousness, as a bridegroom decks himself with a garland, and as a bride adorns herself with her jewels. For as the earth brings forth its shoots, and as a garden causes what is sown in it to spring up, so the Lord GOD will cause righteousness and praise to spring up before all the nations.

Comments on the Text

Why do bad things happen to good people? How can an all-powerful God allow bad things to happen to God's devoted followers? These

questions have perplexed people throughout the ages. The writer(s) of
Third Isaiah struggled with these same questions.[1] The kingdom of Judah
and the city of Jerusalem lay in ruins after the Babylonian defeat of the
Jewish kingdom, and the people were scattered and destitute, wondering
why their God had abandoned them. The poverty, violence, and social
upheaval of today's world leave many people asking the same questions:
Where is God and God's promised reign of peace and salvation? Chapter
61 of Isaiah offers hope to all who have been waiting and anticipating
God's promised deliverance.

The poem in chapter 61 is perhaps more well known for its location
in Luke 4:16–19, part of which Jesus read in the synagogue in Nazareth
and then declared, "Today this scripture has been fulfilled in your hearing" (Luke 4:21). The intended meaning of the first three verses of the
poem is not fully clear, but we hear echoes of the Servant Songs (Isaiah
42:1–4; 49:1–6; 50:4–9; 52:13—53:12) in this poem. The servant was to
suffer for the people, but in doing so would bring hope and ultimately
triumph. The servant in this poem has been called by God, "the spirit of
the Lord God is upon me, because the Lord has anointed me" (61:1), to
fulfill a mission, "he has sent me" (61:1). The question then becomes, who
is the servant? John McKenzie argues that the poet "thinks of himself as
fulfilling the mission of the Servant, and thus he becomes an early interpreter of the Servant Songs."[2] This understanding of the poet and the
poet's intentions seems to make sense, since the mission of "the servant" is
not addressed to an individual, but is addressed to the whole of God's
people. The "you" in verse 5–7 is plural, indicating that it is not a single
person's flock that will be fed, or land that will be tilled, but a whole
nation's, the people of God.

The mission of the servant of God is to proclaim the promised salvation. The mission of the servant then is to be carried out by the people of
God. The oppressed, the brokenhearted, the captives, the prisoners, and
"all who mourn" are to be brought the "good news" of "liberty" and
"release" (61:1). The promised salvation is brought about not by the power
and might of God, but by the "oaks of righteousness" (61:3). Salvation is
dependent on the right actions of each person to every other person, and
perhaps to all of creation.

Beginning in v. 6, the mission is expanded from bringing the "good
news" to only the children of Israel, to include bringing the good news to
all the people of the world. The children of Israel are to be the "priests of
the Lord" and the "ministers of our God" (61:6). The people of God are
to act as mediators between God and "the nations" (61:6). The position of
priest in ancient Judah and Israel was an important and vital position.

Only the priests were able to offer sacrifice and prayer in the name of the people and were the ones who presented and explained the law of God. Just as the priests theoretically have no need to worry about their material needs, Israel will also not have to worry about its needs. The nations will care for Israel's needs while they fulfill God's mission, just as the people care for the priest's needs. The mission to bring the promised salvation is not limited only to Israel, but the promised salvation of God is for all the nations. When the servant of the Lord has successfully completed the mission, then "righteousness and praise [will] spring up before all the nations" (61:11).

The season of Advent is one of anticipation. We hopefully anticipate the arrival of the servant who will usher in God's promised salvation. The servant of the Lord is all those who "love justice" (61:8) and who "bring good news to the oppressed," "brokenhearted," "the captives," and "the prisoners" (61:1). When all of God's children recognize and take their place as God's servants, then we, too, can proclaim, "Today this scripture has been fulfilled in your hearing"(Luke 4:21).

CHILDREN'S SERMON ━━━━━━━━━━━━━━━━━━━━━━

The Tinker King

There was once a young king who disliked the ceremony and trappings of being king. He reluctantly wore a crown and was uncomfortable when forced to sit on the throne. It began the day of his coronation when they brought him a magnificent mink robe. "Where did this robe come from?" asked the young king.

The official replied, "It came from the royal merchant, your highness."

"Where did this robe come from?" the king repeated.

"Why, it came from Persia," the confused official replied.

"Where did this robe come from?" the king insisted.

Finally the official blurted, "Majesty, this robe comes from the skin of small animals whom the hunters trap!"

Sadly, the king touched the robe and said, "How can I wear such cruelty for a robe?"

Another time a prince brought a pearl of immense value to the king as a gift. When the prince gave him the pearl, the king asked the prince, "Why is this pearl so valuable?"

"Because of its perfect, moon-like shape," replied the prince.

But the king asked again, "Why is this pearl so valuable?"

"Because it comes from the depth of the ocean," replied the prince.

Again the king insisted, "Why is this pearl so valuable?"

Finally the flustered prince confessed, "This pearl is valuable because sixteen slaves drowned while trying to retrieve it from the ocean floor."

Sadly, the king refused the gift saying, "How can I wear such cruelty for a jewel?"

The people said the king was too sensitive and gentle to be king, and the king agreed. Then one day the king simply walked away from the palace and never returned.

Soon after, a group of cruel knights replaced the gentle king. They increased the taxes and lived a life of luxury. As the taxes rose, the service deteriorated. Roads and bridges were no longer repaired, and trash and garbage lined the streets.

Meanwhile the king became a tinker and traveled about the country sharpening knives and fixing pots and pans. The people loved the little man who listened with his eyes and asked questions with his heart. The tinker and the people learned from each other.

He learned that the people were unhappy. He learned that the taxes of the knights created a terrible burden, and their inept rule made life difficult.

The people learned from the tinker that everything is connected to everything else and that whenever anything dies a little, we all die a lot. But the people never learned that he was really the king.

One day he was sharpening knives at the house of a family whose son had died in the fields while working long hours, trying to earn enough money to pay the monthly taxes. The tinker asked the father a question, "Who did this to your son?"

"The heat did it; the heat killed my son," the man replied sadly.

Again the tinker asked the man, "Who did this to your son?"

"The long hours with no rest killed my son," replied the father.

But the tinker insisted, "Who did this to your son?"

"The knights did this. The cruel knights killed my boy!" cried the father.

"What are we to do?" the boy's father pleaded. But the tinker did not reply. "You see connections," he cried. "You make us see connections with your questions. Now that we see, what are we to do?"

Looking up from the knife he was sharpening on his wheel, the tinker said quietly, "The knights have not always ruled this kingdom. One day they will be removed."

As the father and the tinker talked, a crowd had gathered to listen to the kindhearted tinker.

"How can we fight men with swords," a woman in the crowd asked, "when all we have are farming tools?"

The tinker stood and faced the crowd. He spoke with a voice that was powerful and clear, "When the time comes, you will not use swords. All that will be needed will be stout poles. Begin now to collect them."

"Before we collect our poles," a voice shouted, "answer one question. Are you the king?"

But the tinker did not answer. He simply waved his hand and left.

A few days later the tinker stopped by the side of the road near the royal palace to work on his cart, and a knight rode up beside him.

"What are you doing, you old fool?" the knight bellowed.

"I am sharpening knives," replied the tinker.

"Are you a tinker?" snorted the knight.

"I am," answered the tinker.

"Then you are coming with me," the knight said triumphantly.

The knight tied a rope around the tinker and dragged him into the royal courtyard. The knight then yelled for all to hear. "Brothers, noble knights. I have brought a tinker to sharpen our weapons. Bring your swords and axes, and the tinker will put a fine edge on all our steel."

For three long days the tinker worked, sharpening the weapons of the cruel rulers. Every blade in the palace was sharpened. When the tinker had finished, the swords were so sharp that they could cut fine paper. The big knight pushed the tinker out through the city gates and jeered, "We have spared your life so that you can sharpen our weapons another day."

Quickly the tinker went about the nearby villages and called the people together. "The time has come. Gather at dawn tomorrow outside the palace and bring your stout poles."

Before the sun rose all the people of the kingdom gathered near the castle where the knights lived. Each carried a stout pole or farming tool. In front of them stood the tinker.

When the great doors of the castle opened, the knights appeared in all their armor, swords in hand. As the knights began to move, fear seized the crowd.

"Stand tall, my people," shouted the tinker.

"But we are about to die," the people shouted.

"No," the tinker insisted, "you are about to live. Do not strike these men. They are your poorest sons. Only stop their swords with your sticks."

No one understood what the tinker meant, but they trusted him and stood firm. The knights roared with laughter at the sight of the peasants facing them with sticks. The first knight went straight for the tinker and swung his sword right at the head of the tinker. But as the sword hit the wooden pole, instantly the sword crumbled into a thousand pieces. You see, the tinker, in sharpening the knight's swords to such a fine edge, had ground away their substance. The swords were sharp to the eye and soft to the touch, but when they met wood, they withered like tissue.

One by one the knights were disarmed. Without a single death, without a single injury, the battle was over.

All the people gathered around the tinker and cheered. One old man spoke, asking, "Tell us once and for all, are you the king?"

The tinker answered, "I am." The people began to cheer and shout, "Crown the tinker king, crown the tinker king!"

Holding up his hands for quiet, the tinker said, "I am not a king who will rule over you. I have come not to be served, but to serve. I have come to help you see that everything is connected to everything else. I urge you to choose leaders who love justice and who live humbly and simply. Remember, the greatest among you must be a servant to all." Then he slipped away and let them begin a new life.[3]

Reflections on the Story

It is a great temptation during Advent to look for stories with a "Christmas" theme. Even the children in the audience at this time of year are expecting Christmas stories. At school they are working on Christmas projects, and they are watching almost nightly, during the Advent season, Christmas specials. Everywhere they look they see Christmas. But if part of our task during the children's sermon is teach the children in our care the traditions of the church, we cannot succumb to the temptation of doing Christmas stories during Advent. Instead, we should help the children to develop their sense of anticipation and wonder at the coming of Jesus. This hopeful anticipation is the focus of both the third week of Advent and Isaiah 61.

"The Tinker King" contains many of these elements. It is a story of a king who does not simply leave the people to live a life of hopelessness and despair, but who comes to really live with and for the people of his kingdom and, when all seems lost, then returns as the king. But like God, the king does not return to rule over the people, but returns to teach the people how they should live and be servants to all. The Isaiah text reminds the hearer that God does not only intervene to "bring good news to the oppressed, to bind up the brokenhearted" (61:1) and "to comfort all who mourn" (61:2), but also provides the framework for a better way—"the oil of gladness" and "righteousness" (61:3, 11). "The Tinker King" also reminds the hearer of these same things. The tinker king comforts the father whose son dies in the field, but instead of taking power when the people offer the kingdom to him, he refuses, reminding them of all that he has taught them: seek justice, humility, and simplicity, and remember that everything is connected to everything else.

NOTES

¹ Scholars have commonly divided the book of Isaiah into three sections: First Isaiah, chapters 1–39, written prior to the Babylonian exile, ca. 700 B.C.E.; Second Isaiah, chapters 40–55, written during the exile, ca. 551–539 B.C.E.; and Third Isaiah, chapters 56–66, written immediately after the "return" from exile after 539 B.C.E. Anthony R. Ceresko, *Introduction to the Old Testament: A Liberation Perspective* (Maryknoll, New York: Orbis Books, 1992), p. 189f.

² John L. McKenzie, *Second Isaiah* (Garden City, New York: Doubleday, 1986), p. 181.

³ A Western European folktale.

3

The Rabbit Dance

Luke 2:21–24   **First Week of Christmas, Year A**

After eight days had passed, it was time to circumcise the child; and he was called Jesus, the name given by the angel before he was conceived in the womb.

When the time came for their purification according to the law of Moses, they brought him to Jerusalem to present him to the Lord (as it is written in the law of the Lord, "Every firstborn male shall be designated as holy to the Lord"), and they offered a sacrifice according to what is stated in the law of the Lord, "a pair of turtledoves or two young pigeons."

Comments on the Text

The saying goes, "The only thing we have to do is die and pay taxes." Unfortunately, there is quite a bit of truth in this statement for contemporary America today. Ritual and tradition play little or no part in most people's lives. Yet, ritual has played a much more important role in the lives of other societies, including the Jewish society of Jesus and his family. In this short story, the writer of Luke reminds the reader that ritual not only was important in Jesus' community, but is critical to understanding who Jesus was.

Nowhere in any of the four Gospel stories is the point made more strongly or clearly that Jesus and his family were strict and devout followers of Judaism. The fact that Jesus was Jewish and understood the "law of Moses" permeates all the Gospel stories, but in this short story we are told no less than five times that what was being done in the temple was "according to" or "required by the law of the Lord" (including the Simeon and Anna stories and the conclusion to the temple story at 2:39–40).[1] The importance of ritual and tradition is even more clearly understood when we remember who the Lukan audience was. Unlike Matthew, John, and most likely Mark, which were written to Jewish/Christian communities, Luke was written to a Gentile community whose comprehension and understanding of "the Law" would have been limited. Yet, none of these writers "sets Jesus and the church so thoroughly within Judaism, until rejected, as does Luke."[2]

Three rituals are presented in this story: circumcision, purification, and dedication. Although the circumcision story does not take place in the temple and is not fully part of the story, I have included it in the discussion to strengthen the argument. The first ritual is the circumcision of male children. Jesus is circumcised on the eighth day after his birth according to Jewish tradition and law (Gen. 17:12; Lev. 12:3; Luke 1:59; Phil. 3:5). The circumcision marks Jesus' acceptance into the covenant community of God. Jesus' circumcision demonstrates that he was not an outsider tearing down the Jewish hierarchy but was an insider who knew the meaning of the law and not just the letter of the law. It also points out the devotion and adherence of Jesus' parents to the law.

The other two rituals noted in this story are the purification of the mother after childbirth (forty days after the birth in the case of a male child and eighty days in the case of a female child [Lev. 12:1–8]) and the dedication of the child to God. The purification rite calls for the sacrifice of a sheep and a turtledove or pigeon, or if the family cannot afford a sheep, then two turtle doves or two pigeons can be used (Lev. 12:6–8). The Luke story, however, does not mention the required sheep, only the required birds. That Joseph offered two birds in sacrifice for Mary's purification instead of the sheep follows the Lukan theme of Jesus and his family as poor and Jesus' affinity for the poor and outcast.[3]

The dedication of the child to God was a rite reminding the people of the exodus (Ex. 13:2, 11–16). The firstborn male child was to be "redeemed" at a price of five shekels (Num. 18:15–16). However, the writer makes no mention of Jesus' redemption, perhaps because of the writer's lack of or insufficient knowledge about the law, and "instead he [Jesus] is received into the service of God."[4] Whether this is the case or the author had another motive, there are definite parallels to the dedication of Samuel in this story (1 Sam. 1:24–28; 2:20–22). Eduard Schweizer contends that "a prescribed ritual takes on new meaning as a kind of 'presentation' of the newborn child."[5] In both stories the births are promised beforehand (Luke 1:31 and 1 Sam. 1:17). The second parallel is that just as Hannah and Elkanah brought Samuel to the sanctuary and dedicated him to Yahweh (1 Sam. 1:24–28), Mary and Joseph bring Jesus to the temple for dedication. The third parallel is the blessing of the child by a holy man of God. As the story progresses the hearer learns that Simeon blesses Jesus' parents (Luke 2:34) just as Eli had blessed Samuel's (1 Sam. 2:20). The final parallel between the Samuel dedication story and Jesus' dedication story is that the women who ministered at the sanctuary are mentioned. However, it should be noted that Anna, in the Jesus dedication, is described as a prophetess (Luke 2:36) who "praised God" and spoke "of the child to all who were looking for the redemption of Jerusalem" (Luke 2:38). The women in the Samuel story, on the other hand, are described as temple prostitutes "who served at the entrance to the tent of meeting" (1 Sam. 2:22).

Rituals are fading fast in contemporary society. We tend to do things not out of a sense of tradition but out of habit. Why we do what we do and celebrate how we celebrate, are becoming lost. Here in Luke we have a vivid reminder that ritual and tradition are important and help bring understanding to who we are.

CHILDREN'S SERMON ━━━━━━━━━━━━━━━━━━━━━━━━━━

The Rabbit Dance

L ong ago, a group of hunters were out looking for game. They had been hunting all day long but had seen no sign of any animals. Eventually the hunters came to a clearing in the forest. The leader of the hunters held up his hand for the others to stop. He thought he had seen something moving up ahead. All the other men immediately dropped to their stomachs and crept slowly to the edge of the clearing to see what they could see. What they saw amazed them. There, in the center of the clearing, was the biggest rabbit any of them had ever seen. It was as big as a bear!

One of the hunters slowly began to raise his bow, for a rabbit as large as this would provide enough food for the entire village. But the leader of the hunters held out his hand and made a signal with his hand for the man to lower his bow. Something unusual was happening, and it was best to watch and see what would happen next.

The giant rabbit lifted its head and looked straight at the men. Even though they were well hidden on the other side of the clearing, the giant rabbit could see them. Then the rabbit nodded its head, and lifted one of its feet, and thumped the ground, BA–BUM. Rabbits came from the east and the west, from the north and the south, rabbits by the hundreds came until the clearing was filled with rabbits.

Now the giant rabbit began to thump its foot against the ground in a different way. Ba-pum, ba-pum, pa-pum, pa-pum. It was like the sound of a drum beating, ba-pum, ba-pum, pa-pum, pa-pum. The other rabbits made a big circle around the giant rabbit and began to dance. They danced and danced. They danced in couples and moved in and out and back and forth. It was a good dance that the rabbits did. The hunters who were watching found themselves tapping the earth with their hands to the rhythm of the giant rabbit's foot.

Then, suddenly, BA–BUM! The giant rabbit stopped thumping the earth, and all of the rabbits stopped dancing. The chief of the rabbits then leaped high into the air, right over the men's heads, and was gone in a flash. Then all of the other rabbits ran back into the forest in every direction. Just as suddenly as they appeared, they were gone.

The hunters were astonished at what they had seen. None of them had ever seen anything like it before. None of them had ever heard or seen such a dance. All thought of hunting was now gone from their minds. The dance was all they could think or talk about as they went back to the village.

When the hunters reached the village, they went straight to the longhouse where the head of the Clan Mothers lived. Now the Clan Mother was a very wise woman and knew a great deal about the animals. So they told her their story. When they were done telling their story, the Clan Mother picked up a water drum and handed it to the leader of the hunters.

"Play the rhythm that the Rabbit Chief played," she said.

The leader of the men did as she asked. He played the rhythm of the rabbit's dance.

"This is a good sound," said the Clan Mother. "Now show me the dance that the Rabbit People showed you," she said to the other hunters.

The hunters danced while their leader played the drum. The Clan Mother listened closely and watched. When they were done, she smiled at them.

"I understand what has happened," she said. "The Rabbit People know that we rely on them. We hunt them for food and for clothing. The Rabbit Chief has given us this special dance so that we can honor Rabbit People for all that they give to the human beings. If we play their song and do their dance, then they will know we are grateful for all they continue to give us. We must call this new song The Rabbit Dance and we must all do it, men and women together, to honor the Rabbit People."

So it was that a new dance was given to the Iroquois people. To this day the Rabbit Dance is done to thank the Rabbit People for all they have given, not only food and clothing, but also a fine dance that makes the people happy.[6]

Reflections on the Story

I have attempted to use a wide variety of stories from all over the world, from as many different cultures as possible. In doing this I have not specifically looked for any story from any particular culture, except for this story. All cultures have their stories about why things are and how they came about, but Native Americans have been especially vigorous in protecting and preserving their rituals and traditions. The hundreds of different Native cultures in the United States have been in decline since 1492 C. E. Entire societies have been eliminated, but since the 1960s a resurgence in cultural identity has occurred, and the rich stories and rituals have begun anew.

Ritual and religious requirements have fallen on hard times in contemporary society. But, like Judaism and Native American religions, praise of God in all things is essential. In "The Rabbit Dance" we are reminded to be thankful and to praise God for the gift of even the smallest creatures for what they have done for humankind. Praise and thanksgiving in the form of a ritual dance and song are given to God "for not only food and clothing, but a fine dance that makes the people happy." The Iroquois, just as Mary and Joseph, follow the prescribed ritual and in the end are blessed.

NOTES

[1] Fred B. Craddock, *Luke* (Louisville: John Knox Press, 1990), p. 38. Also see R. Alan Culpepper, "The Gospel of Luke," in *The New Interpreter's Bible*, vol. 9 (Nashville: Abingdon Press, 1995), p. 69.

[2] Craddock, *Luke*, p. 37.

[3] Culpepper, "The Gospel of Luke," p. 70.

[4] Eduard Schweizer, *The Good News According to Luke*, translated by David E. Green (Atlanta: John Knox Press, 1984), p. 55.

[5] Ibid.

[6] An Iroquois Native American folktale.

4

The Great Race of the Birds and Animals

Mark 1:2–8   **Week 1 of Epiphany, Year B**

As it is written in the prophet Isaiah,

"See, I am sending my messenger ahead of you, who will prepare your way; the voice of one crying out in the wilderness: 'Prepare the way of the Lord, make his paths straight,'"

John the baptizer appeared in the wilderness, proclaiming a baptism of repentance for the forgiveness of sins. And people from the whole Judean countryside and all the people of Jerusalem were going out to him, and were baptized by him in the river Jordan, confessing their sins. Now John was clothed with camel's hair, with a leather belt around his waist, and he ate locusts and wild honey. He proclaimed, "The one who is more powerful than I is coming after me; I am not worthy to stoop down and untie the thong of his sandals. I have baptized you with water; but he will baptize you with the Holy Spirit."

Comments on the Text

Most people just love to hear "good news." This is usually because the good news has in some way saved someone or something from some fate or another. When one is in college, or when young couples first start out, good news is an unexpected check or cash windfall that staves off the creditors for another day. Good news can be the announcement of a birth or the cure of a disease. In almost every case news is not defined as "good" unless the news is about someone being saved from something. This text is the story of "the beginning of the good news of Jesus Christ, the Son of God" (Mark 1:1), declaring that God is involved in the work of salvation in the past (the prophecies of Isaiah and Malachi; 1:2–3), the present (John appeared in the desert preaching and baptizing those who came; 1:4–5), and the future (one will come after and will baptize with the Holy Spirit; 1:7–8). Lamar Williamson states it this way: "From God's promises in the past the text moves to John's call for his hearers to respond in the present and to his announcement of what God is about to do in the future."[1]

The Mark author immediately connects the "good news" of Jesus with Old Testament salvation prophecies. The author of Mark attributes the quotation in verses 2 and 3 to the prophet Isaiah; however, the text is really a combination of Malachi and Isaiah. The passage combines the promised messenger who will prepare God's way from Malachi 3:1 and Isaiah 40:3's promised way of salvation from the wilderness. The reader is reminded that "salvation traditionally comes from the wilderness. Moses, Elijah, and David all had to flee to the wilderness (Ex. 2:15; 1 Sam. 23:14; 1 Kings 19:3–4). Likewise, Jesus will emerge from the wilderness to begin preaching the good news and will return there several times (Mark 1:35, 45; 6:31–32, 35; 8:4)."[2] It is from the barren, deserted, and uninhabitable places that God has brought forth, is bringing forth, and will bring forth salvation for God's people.

The Malachi text alludes to a messenger who will prepare the way for God. Traditionally, this preparing messenger was thought to be Elijah, who was to return just before the end times. The connection between John and Elijah is clear at verse 6, where John is described in virtually the same terms as Elijah: "A hairy man, with a leather belt around his waist." (2 Kings 1:8). John's diet of "locusts and wild honey" also distinguishes him as a prophet in the Old Testament tradition. Whether John was considered to be Elijah returned or not is not of importance. What is important is that John was clearly understood as the forerunner of Jesus who went "ahead" and prepared the "way" (1:2). The Mark writer has also reworded Malachi 3:1. This rewording of Malachi is not accidental but intentional. In Malachi the messenger prepares the way for YHWH, "LORD." Here in Mark, the messenger prepares the way for the one who is "coming after" (1:7). The hearers of Mark remember that the one who goes ahead and prepares the way is the forerunner of the Lord. In its reworked state the hearers of the gospel recognize that Jesus is the one who is "coming after" (1:7). Therefore, Jesus cannot be just another prophet, but is in fact Lord.[3]

John preaches in the wilderness a "baptism of repentance for the forgiveness of sins" (1:4). Williamson contends that "the context makes it plain that John preaches and baptizes, the hearers [those that come to hear John preach] sin and repent, and God forgives."[4] If, as the author contends, the Old Testament prophecies have been fulfilled, then a special time of salvation is being inaugurated that depends on repentance. The Greek word translated as "repentance" literally means a "change of mind" and is used to translate the Hebrew word to "return." The prophets of the Old Testament, many times, called the people to return to God. "Therefore, it is not the changing of the characteristics and actions of a person that is emphasized, but the transformation of the total direction of that life, that is, of the person's relationship to God."[5]

Because those who came to John "confessed their sins" (1:5), repentance involves not only the change of direction in a person's life, but the acknowledgment or recognition of their sins. Others contend that repentance causes a person to confess his or her sins. This chicken or the egg argument, however, seems to be of little consequence. The call to repentance from a prophet was nothing new to the people of Israel. Prophets in the Old Testament continually called for national repentance. These calls for the people to come together and repent are commonly described as a "prelude to the 'day of the Lord'—that is the day when God will judge the nation for its sin."[6] The main emphasis for us to consider is that salvation includes both repentance and confession, and repentance *is* "preparation for the Lord's coming."[7]

In some sense the Christian rite of baptism is different from the Jewish baptismal rites of Jesus' time. Yet, at their very heart is the concept of purification. As Christians we tend to think that baptism is a strictly Christian ritual, intiated by John baptizing Jesus. However, the ritual purification by water is an ancient custom. The difference between the two can be located in verse 8. Where the baptism of John and other Jewish baptisms of water required continual renewal and needed to be done periodically, the baptism offered those who follow the "more powerful" (1:7) one to come is a once-and-for-all baptism of purification. The call to repentance, forgiveness, and purification by John then is a warning that the day of the Lord, that is, the day of judgement, is fast coming.

The central issue of the story is found in verses 7–8. John and his baptism of water are not what is important, as the author indicates by John's own understanding of unworthiness compared to the one who "is coming after" (1:7). The importance is found in the "more powerful" one to come, the one who will baptize not with water, but with the "Holy Spirit" (1:8). The baptism of the Holy Spirit indicates that the turning away of repentance will be "a permanent change in an individual's relationship with God."[8] The Mark story reminds us that the reign of God has begun but is not yet complete. In hopeful anticipation we wait for the coming of the one "more powerful" who will bring the complete baptism. Yet, at the same time we are called to return to the Lord God and live our lives in accord with God.

CHILDREN'S SERMON ────────────────────────────

The Great Race of the Birds and Animals

L ong ago, when the world was still quite new, buffalos used to eat people, instead of people eating buffalos.

The people did not like being eaten, so they began to pray and asked the Creator to end their suffering. The Creator saw how the people suffered and heard their prayers for help. So one day the Creator asked Crow to call all living things together to the mountains that touch the clouds in the center of the great plains. The people and the buffalos and every bird and animal heard Crow calling, and they came to the mountains from all directions across the plains.

The Creator stood on the highest mountaintop and spoke to all the creatures: "*Toke*. Is it right that buffalos eat people? Or should people eat buffalos instead?" the Creator asked. "All the tribes of four-legged and winged animals will decide. There will be a great race around these mountains. If the buffalos' team wins the race, they will still eat people. But if the people's team wins the race, they will eat the buffalos instead. Get ready. Choose your fastest runners. Join the side you want to win."

The people chose a young man. He had never lost a race. Even the buffalos knew he would be hard to beat, but they had a young cow to run for them. She was everyone's favorite, and they were sure she would win.

The animals joined with the buffalos, because they have four legs. The birds sided with the people, because they have two legs, like we do. Each tribe of animals chose its fastest runner.

All the racers gathered at the foot of the mountain, when suddenly Wolf and Coyote raised their heads and h-o-w-l-e-d. *Hoowllllll!* The runners sped away with a thunder of feet and great wind of flying birds.

The birds flew ahead like arrows, all, that is, but little Magpie. Magpie beat her wings as fast as she could, but no matter how hard she tried even the tiniest birds left her behind. But Magpie had made up her mind she was going to win the race. She had been thinking things out and had come up with a plan. She swooped down very quietly and landed on Buffalo's back.

The day was very hot. The birds were panting, and when they came to a stream they stopped to drink. But they drank too much and soon fell asleep in the trees. The animals swam past them; except for Beaver, whose legs were too short for such a long race, and he slipped into a lovely pool in the shade of the trees. Otter followed, and Muskrat, too.

Buffalo and the young man took the lead; the larger animals were staying close behind. Jack-Rabbit was hopping along well until he saw Coyote trotting behind him; he became so frightened that he fled out into the plains, where he is still running, always wondering who is behind him.

Nobody remembers how long they raced around the mountains, but it was several days. Tired runners dropped out all along the way. Prairie Dog wasted his energy chattering at Hawk. Rattlesnake ate Toad and then curled up to sleep. Mouse vanished down a hole when Bear almost stepped on her. Mole and Gopher tunneled along underground, and even to this day they think the race is still on.

Slowly, mile by mile, Buffalo took the lead, and the young man fell further and further behind. He had run his very best, but he was nearly spent and could not catch Buffalo. Even Buffalo was almost exhausted as her head hung low. But when Buffalo saw the finish line, she ran faster in a final burst of energy. Faster and faster she ran, and all the four-legged animals watching from the mountainside cheered her on. They were quite sure she was the winner. Faster and faster, closer and closer Buffalo ran.

Suddenly Magpie flew up from Buffalo's back. Everyone had forgotten about her! She was was well rested and was not tired at all! Magpie flew straight up toward the sun. And then she swooped down, squawking and squawking, and crossed the finish line just in front of Buffalo. There was a shout like thunder as the people and birds cheered Magpie's victory.

Magpie, the slowest of all the birds, had won the race for the two-legged animals! The chief of the Buffalo nation told the people: "You have won the race fairly. Now we are under your power. You will eat us."

And the Creator spoke to the people and warned them: "Use your power wisely. Look after all things that I have made, even the smallest of them. For they are all your relatives. Make yourselves worthy of them, and give thanks always."

After that the people were shown how to make bows and arrows and were given horses by the Creator. They used their powers wisely, never hunting the buffalos for sport, but only when they needed meat.

The people have always been grateful to the birds for taking their side in the Great Race. And this is why they wear the birds' beautiful feathers, so that they may honor them.[9]

Reflections on the Story

Locating a story that will help children understand salvation and the need to turn to God is not an easy task. For most Christians the word salvation is usually associated only with the notion of resurrection and entry into heaven. This concept is difficult for most adults to get a handle on, let alone for a child. I have searched for a story that has people seeking salvation from a problem. In this story the solution to the problem, or salvation, means that the people will live. Life, after all, is the point of Christian salvation.

"The Great Race of the Birds and Animals" is a wonderful story of salvation. The people are being eaten and destroyed by the buffalo and are in need of salvation. In the people's search for salvation they "turn" to God, "the Creator," and ask for a change. To prepare the way for salvation, the Creator calls for a race that includes all of creation. Ultimately, salvation is gained for the people because the birds, in particular the magpie, choose to join the people. To honor the birds and to remember how the birds prepared the way in the wilderness, the people wear bird feathers. The people of the story find salvation only when they willingly turn to God, just as we all can.

NOTES

[1] Lamar Williamson, Jr., *Mark* (Louisville: John Knox Press, 1983), p. 30.

[2] Pheme Perkins, "The Gospel of Mark," in *The New Interpreter's Bible*, vol. 8 (Nashville: Abingdon Press, 1995), p. 530f.

[3] Ibid., p. 531.

[4] Williamson, *Mark*, p. 31.

[5] Eduard Schweizer, *The Good News According to Mark*, translated by David E. Green (Atlanta: John Knox Press, 1974), p. 32 (altered to be inclusive); also see Williamson, *Mark*, p. 31, and Perkins, "The Gospel of Mark," p. 531.

[6] Perkins, "The Gospel of Mark," p. 531.

[7] Williamson, *Mark*, p. 32.

[8] Perkins, "The Gospel of Mark," p. 532.

[9] A Cheyenne Native American story.

5

Three Stone Woman

Isaiah 40:25–31   **Week 5 of Epiphany, Year B**

To whom then will you compare me, or who is my equal? says the Holy One. Lift up your eyes on high and see: Who created these? He who brings out their host and numbers them, calling them all by name; because he is great in strength, mighty in power, not one is missing.

Why do you say, O Jacob, and speak, O Israel, "My way is hidden from the Lord, and my right is disregarded by my God"? Have you not known? Have you not heard? The Lord is the everlasting God, the Creator of the ends of the earth. He does not faint or grow weary; his understanding is unsearchable. He gives power to the faint, and strengthens the powerless. Even youths will faint and be weary, and the young will fall exhausted; but those who wait for the Lord shall renew their strength, they shall mount up with wings like eagles, they shall run and not be weary, they shall walk and not faint.

Comments on the Text

Life is never easy, even for children. Problems spring up constantly that try our patience and wear us out, both physically and emotionally. No matter how hard we try to eliminate problems or try to avoid situations that could cause us problems, problems still find us. Happiness and peace are not found in avoiding difficulties but are found in how we deal with and overcome the adversities that bog us down. Between 587 and 539 B. C. E. the Hebrew community of Palestine faced the difficulty of coping with the loss of their promised land and Davidic monarchy to the outsiders from Babylon. The nation state was destroyed, and by common understanding within the ancient Near Eastern world, the people understood that the power of Yahweh was either dead, or at the very least that the power of Yahweh was not equal to that of the Babylonian's supreme god, Marduk. Second Isaiah, more commonly called Deutero-Isaiah, writes this oracle of hope to help the people cope with the anxieties and fears created by the socio-political upheaval of conquest.

With the destruction of the kingdom and the removal of the hierarchy to far-off Babylon, many doubted their God: "How could God just abandon them in their time of need?" or "Could Marduk be more powerful than Yahweh?" The writer begins this oracle with God asking, "To whom then will you compare me, or who is my equal?" (Isaiah 40:25). God immediately understands the doubts of those who are God's followers and points out that God is the Creator (Isaiah 40:26).[1] Yahweh is the one who created the heavens and the earth. The Creator is so intimately tied to the creation that God not only knows their "number," but God knows them "all by name" (40:26). The implication here is that if God knows the uncountable number of stars in the sky, then how much more does God know about each of God's chosen people? The Israelites are suffering trials and tribulations, and although it may seem that they have been abandoned, the God who knows the stars by name is still with God's people.

The Isaiah writer then demonstrates that it is all of God's people who are confused and frightened. Jacob is the term used by all the Isaiah writers to signify the Northern Kingdom, and the word Israel the Southern Kingdom. It would appear that the writer is including both the North and the South in the people's lament regarding where God is. This is important to note and remember. Because Deutero-Isaiah includes all of God's people in the lament that "my way is hidden from the LORD, and my right is disregarded by my God" (40:27), the writer is also including all of God's people in the promise of God's renewing power and strength (40:29). However, it would be a stretch, and extremely unfaithful to the text, to assume that the writer is making a statement concerning God's universalism.

The prophet outlines the Israelites' anxieties and fears in verse 27. The author then reminds the Israelites of what they know and have heard about God but have forgotten in their time of trouble. Just as God is in full control of the heavens, God is in full control of the descendants of

Jacob. This could be another possible reason that the writer uses the call of Jacob and Israel in verse 27. By using the names of the patriarch of the nation, the people are reminded that God made an everlasting covenant with God's people, a covenant that cannot be broken by an earthly power.[2] This idea is reinforced in verse 28, where the prophet also reminds the people that Yahweh is not only the God of the covenant through the patriarchs, but is the God of creation and is "the everlasting God" (40:28). The prophet appeals to the traditional precepts of the faith, that God is a covenantal God and is the creator of all. These are used to reassure the disillusioned, confused Israelites that God has not abandoned them but is strong and powerful, although God is mysterious and "his understanding is unsearchable" (40:28) for human beings. It is not that God has not or does not hear the cries of God's people, but how and when God works is unfathomable for human beings.

"Weary" and "faint" occur three times in the final section of the oracle. The first time in verse 28 is a reminder that God does not grow weary or faint. The second (40:29) and the third (40: 31) time is a reminder that God gives to those who need it the strength and power not to grow weary or faint. In a bold statement the prophet states emphatically that God gives power and strength to humankind. The Hebrew participle "giving" indicates that God's help is not a once-in-a-while help but is always characteristic of God.[3] The contrast between God and humanity is demonstrated clearly in verse 30. Unlike God, who is inexhaustible, humanity even at its peak physical state—"youths" and "young"—can be and is worn out. "But those who wait for the LORD shall renew their strength" (40:31). We tend to think of the word "wait" as a passive word. If we are to wait we do nothing until we are called for. But in Hebrew the word means to "wait with confident, expectation, trust"[4] The renewal of strength and power, then, is given to those who are confident and trust in God.

Through faith God gives those who wait the strength to continue on the path of life. The eagle throughout antiquity was a symbol of great strength and power and is used metaphorically here to convey the magnitude of encouragement and strength God can mete out. The encouragement is such that no longer will the believer wearily crawl through life but will be strengthened so that she or he is able to run along life's path, climbing over the trials and tribulations that spring up along the way.

Three Stone Woman

L ong ago Ana lived with her four children far to the north on the Alaskan Island of Little Diomede. Ana's husband had been killed in a hunting accident, and she had no one to hunt for her. When the little food she had left after her husband was killed ran out, Ana decided to go to her brother-in-law, Tikik, and his wife, Tula, to ask for some food. Tikik and Tula lived on the other side of the island. Because the winter winds had already begun to blow, the trip was very dangerous through the snow and ice. But without food Ana and her children would die.

When Ana arrived at the home of Tikik and Tula she was met by Tula.

"Please, just a little food," Ana begged. "Anything you have to spare. My children are starving."

But Tula was a cold-hearted woman and said, "And what are your children to me? Look around you; the whole village is starving. Go away. We have nothing to spare."

Now, Tikik had a kind heart and loved his brother's wife and children, so when he heard what Tula said, he became very angry with his wife. "You are a cruel woman," he said. "We have more than enough. Go to the cold storage and give my brother's children some food."

Tula went to the cold storage, but she did not go with a good heart. Quickly she filled a sack and set it outside for Ana. "There is your food," she said. "Take it and go."

Ana bid her brother and sister-in-law good-bye and began the long walk home. As she trudged through the heavy snow Ana noticed how heavy the sack was. "My sister-in-law is good after all," she thought. "We will eat well the rest of the winter with what Tula has given us."

Ana did not stop until she was in the middle of the island. There she rested for a moment and looked into the bag.

Inside the bag she saw nothing but three large stones.

Ana wept, for without food she and her children would starve.

Crying, she went on, leaving the bag of stones behind.

It was becoming dark, and the wind blew hard and cold. So when Ana came to a small cave, she decided to go in and rest. When she entered the cave she was surprised to see two strangers there. The strangers made room for her in the cave. One of the strangers spoke and said, "You look cold and tired."

"I am," said the weary Ana.

"Why do you travel in such weather?" asked the other.

"To seek food for my children," said Ana.

And then she told the strangers the story of the stones.

The strangers' hearts went out to Ana and her children.

"We can give you some food," said one, reaching into his parka. What he brought out was the tiniest sealskin poke (bag) Ana had ever seen. He placed it in her hands, and said, "Take this home and put it in your cold storage. Be sure that it is well cushioned and has a lot of room around it. Then go to sleep with your children. You can sleep for a long time or for a short time. And then when you wake, go to your cold storage and see what has become of the sealskin poke. Go now and do as I say."

Ana went straight home. When she arrived she did just as the man had said. She cushioned the sealskin poke in her empty cold storage and went to bed.

When she awoke, she and her children went to the cold storage and found that the tiny sealskin poke was full of seal oil, seal meat, and seal blubber, more than enough for a meal. And after they had eaten their fill, the poke was still full.

Soon Ana and her children were fat and strong. Ana did not hoard her treasure but shared the bounty of food with the others in her village. And still there was enough for all.

Warmer days came. And with them came Tikik and his dog team. He came to visit his sister-in-law and his brother's children.

"You did not come for more food," he said to Ana. "I worried that you might starve."

"We did not starve," said Ana, "but it is not because of Tula." And she told him of the stones.

"You are a brave woman, sister-in-law," said Tikik. "But Tula is a cruel woman. You and your children will never go hungry again, for I will hunt for you and your children forever."

And he set off across the snow to hunt for Ana and the children of his brother, who were never hungry again.[5]

Reflections on the Story

Life is full of obstacles and roadblocks. Time and again problems bog us down, discourage us, and wear us out. In looking for a story for this text I found the most critical element that a story had to have was a character who was overburdened with a misery but who, even at the most critical point, the point where most people would give up, found the strength and courage to continue. "Three Stone Woman" is a story that can help young children understand that even in the bleakest times God is still with us, and in persevering we can cope with the problems that interrupt our lives.

Three Stone Woman is faced with the ultimate problem—survival. She has no one to hunt for food and is faced with the possibility of her and her children's starving to death in the middle of winter. In her desperation she decides to brave the winter weather and cross the island to seek the help of her brother and sister-in-law. The sister-in-law, instead of giving Three Stone Woman food, gives her a bag with three large stones. Discouraged and confused, Three Stone Woman walks on after discovering the trick that has been played on her. Tired and on the verge of collapsing, Three Stone Woman seeks shelter, where she meets two strangers. The strangers give her a small poke and instructions to follow. With this small encouragement, Three Stone Woman's strength is renewed and she continues home. When Three Stone Woman reaches home she must wait with confidence, expectation, and trust that what the strangers had told her would happen. And, of course, her faith is rewarded and her family not only survives but becomes "fat and strong." In the face of adversity it is easy to think that God has forgotten us, but if we are willing to put our trust in God, we will be given the strength to cope with the difficulties of life.

NOTES

[1] John L. McKenzie, *Second Isaiah* (Garden City, New York: Doubleday, 1986), p. 23.

[2] George A. F. Knight, *Servant Theology: A Commentary on the Book of Isaiah 40–55* (Grand Rapids: William B. Eerdmans Publishing, 1984), p. 24.

[3] R. N. Whybray, *Isaiah 40–66* (Grand Rapids: William B. Eerdmans Publishing, 1975), p. 59.

[4] Ibid.

[5] A Native Alaskan folktale.

6

Something from Nothing

Genesis 17:1–7, 15–19   **Week 2 of Lent, Year B**

When Abram was ninety-nine years old, the LORD appeared to Abram, and said to him, "I am God Almighty; walk before me, and be blameless. And I will make my covenant between me and you, and will make you exceedingly numerous." Then Abram fell on his face; and God said to him, "As for me, this is my covenant with you: You shall be the ancestor of a multitude of nations. No longer shall your name be Abram, but your name shall be Abraham; for I have made you the ancestor of a multitude of nations. I will make you exceedingly fruitful; and I will make nations of you, and kings shall come from you. I will establish my covenant between me and you, and your offspring after you throughout their generations, for an everlasting covenant, to be God to you and to your offspring after you.

God said to Abraham, "As for Sarai your wife, you shall not call her Sarai, but Sarah shall be her name. I will bless her, and moreover I will give you a son by her. I will bless her, and she shall give rise to nations; kings of peoples shall come from her." Then Abraham fell on his face and laughed, and said to himself, "Can a child be born to a man who is a hundred years old? Can Sarah, who is ninety years old, bear a child?" And Abraham said to God, "O that Ishmael might live in your sight!" God said, "No, but your wife Sarah shall bear you a son, and you shall name him Isaac. I will establish my covenant with him as an everlasting covenant for his offspring after him."

56

Comments on the Text

In contemporary North American society a promise is viewed skeptically. More often than not the only thing anticipated about a promise is when it will be broken. The question of *if* it will be broken is never considered, because everyone knows that it will be. As Christians we are taught from our earliest recollections that faith demands that we not only believe in promises, but that we believe the promises will be kept. Some people are able to do this without any reservation. However, most of us are caught up in our skepticism concerning promises and have to struggle with the guilt of doubt. Fortunately, we are not the only ones who have struggled with promises. Throughout the Bible we meet people who also struggle with believing in promises and that those promises will be kept. Even the patriarch of the Judeo-Christian religion, Abraham, struggled with believing in God's promises.

Chapter 17 is the Priestly writers' version of the Abraham and Sarah covenant story, which the Yahwist's writers previously describe in chapter 15.[1] The importance of this should not be overlooked. The Priestly faction was concerned with the rituals and maintenance of circumcision as the mark of the communities' continued adherence and acceptance of God's covenental promise.[2] This is not to imply that circumcision was the only concern of the Priestly writers, but in the context of this story its importance cannot be discounted. Two other Priestly literary constructions should also be noted: the use of *El Shaddai* and the traditional story pattern of repeated words or phrases in groups of three (or multiples of three) and seven. Scholars are unclear what exactly *El Shaddai* means, but most have tended to use the translation "God Almighty" or "all powerful."[3] The actual meaning of *El Shaddai* is now obscured, but the Priestly writers tended to use this title frequently for God to demonstrate that this is the God of old, the Creator and keeper of all promises.[4]

This covenant story involves the obligations of both God and humanity. God calls Abram to "walk" before God and "be blameless" (Genesis 17:1). In return for following God's directions, Abram is promised numerous descendants (17:2). God's obligation to the covenant is to supply Abram with heir(s), which is reiterated two other times in this story (17:4, 6). Abram's response to God's call is a ritual one. He falls "on his face" (17:3). The act of falling on one's face was an ancient expression of total fidelity and obedience to a superior.[5] Abram submits to the human obligation of the covenant before he even knows what his part of the bargain is. It is not until verse 10 that we, and Abram, learn that the human obligation is the ritual act of circumcision for Abram and all male descendants.

To seal the covenant, or more accurately to symbolize the turning point in a person's life, God changes Abram's name to Abraham. Scholars are divided on what, if any, is the difference between the meaning of these two names. But, within the context of the story it is fair to say that, at the very least, Abraham means "will be the father of many."[6] Even at ninety-nine years old, Abraham will be what God wants him to be, regardless of how preposterous the idea may seem.

The following three verses (17:6–8) spell out exactly what God's promise is and means: God will make Abraham "exceedingly fruitful," "make nations" of Abraham, and "kings will come from" Abraham (17:6). Not only will Abraham have many descendants, but those descendants will be great and powerful according to human standards. The covenant is not limited to Abraham alone but is an "everlasting covenant" (17:7). God will establish this everlasting covenant with Abraham's "offspring… throughout their generations" guaranteeing to be God to Abraham and to all his offspring. This covenantal phrase is another Priestly literary construction meant to demonstrate the special relationship that exists between God and God's covenant partners.[7] The final promise of the covenant is that the descendants will be given "the land where you are now an alien, all the land of Canaan" as "a perpetual holding" (17:8).

This is one of those pericopes that are too much for children to handle in one setting. Because of this, I have opted to follow the lectionary's lead and not include verses 9–14 (the discussion concerning the rite of circumcision). However, to further our understanding of the significance and importance of the whole pericope, it is necessary to look at the human obligation to the covenant established by God. God's obligation to the covenant is to multiply Abraham; Abraham's obligation is to submit to circumcision. Historically we know that other cultures in the region also practiced circumcision, but apparently the Mesopotamian cultures did not. The Priestly writers were actively writing at the time of the Babylonian exile. During the period of the exile circumcision was viewed as a clear sign of who was a true believer and who were the pagan overlords who did not practice circumcision.[8] Circumcision in this story is a sign of the covenant between God and the descendants of Abraham.

Before continuing with this story, we should remember that at this point, Abraham thinks that God is making the promise of progeny and land through his son Ishmael, who was born by Sarai's "slave-girl," Hagar the Egyptian (chapter 16). Now the covenant story begins its third scene, and to Abraham's astonishment, the most absurd and unbelievable promise of God is made in verses 15–16. It is not through the son of Hagar that the promise will be kept, but through the child of ninety-year-old Sarai (17:16). In this act God not only seals the covenant with the Hebrew males, but extends the promise and covenant to include both men and women by changing Sarai's name to Sarah. Sarah receives from God the same covenantal promise that Abraham received in verse 6: God will give the aged, childless couple a son, who will give rise to nations and kings. Abraham's reaction to this promise is the same reaction most people would have: a mixture of surprise, reverence, and disbelief. Upon hearing this promise given to Sarah, Abraham immediately falls on his face to demonstrate his fidelity and obedience. But his doubts about God's ability to keep this promise are betrayed by his laughter and thoughts: "Can a child be born to a man who is a hundred years old? Can Sarah, who is ninety years old, bear a child?" (17:17)

Abraham, in an attempt to steer God back into reality, asks God, "Surely you must mean my son Ishmael?" But this is not God's plan. God's plan is to work through the child of promise that the aged Sarah will bear. It is God who has the last laugh, saying, "No, but your wife Sarah shall bear you a son, and you shall name him Isaac [Hebrew for laughter]" (17:19). Every time Abraham calls his son by name, he will be reminded that nothing is impossible for God. J. Gerald Janzen explains Isaac's naming in this way: "As for Isaac, his name gives him his identity and his vocation. He is the embodiment of that laughter and that questioning which, starting in the human breast as humorous doubt, in God's hands is transformed understanding of the wisdom and the power at the base of nature and society."[9] But even in doubt and questioning, Abraham moves forward and follows the directions and maintains his part of the covenant.

CHILDREN'S SERMON

Something from Nothing

When Joseph was a little baby, his grandfather made him a wonderful blanket to keep him warm and cozy and to help chase away bad dreams.

Joseph loved his wonderful blanket, and took it everywhere he went. But as Joseph grew older, the wonderful blanket grew older, too.

One day his mother said to him, "Joseph, look at your blanket. It's frazzled, it's worn, it's torn and tattered. It is time to throw it out!"

"But Mama, Grandpa can fix it," Joseph said. So Joseph took his blanket to his grandfather.

Grandfather took the blanket and turned it round and round.

"Hmm," he said as his scissors went snip, snap, snip, and his needle went in and out and in and out, "there's just enough material here to make…" a wonderful jacket. Joseph put on the wonderful jacket and went outside to play.

Joseph loved his wonderful jacket and wore it everyday. But as Joseph grew older, the wonderful jacket grew older, too.

One day his mother said to him, "Joseph, look at your jacket. It's shrunken and small, it's torn and tattered, it doesn't fit you at all. It is time to throw it out!"

"But Mama, Grandpa can fix it," Joseph said. So Joseph took his jacket to his grandfather.

Grandfather took the jacket and turned it round and round.

"Hmm," he said as his scissors went snip, snap, snip, and his needle went in and out and in and out, "there's just enough material here to make…" a wonderful vest. Joseph wore the wonderful vest to school the very next day.

Joseph loved his wonderful vest and wore it to school everyday. But as Joseph grew older, the wonderful vest grew older, too.

One day his mother said to him, "Joseph, look at your vest! It's spotted with glue and paint, too, it's torn and tattered. It is time to throw it out!"

"But Mama, Grandpa can fix it," Joseph said. So Joseph took his vest to his grandfather.

Grandfather took the vest and turned it round and round.

"Hmm," he said as his scissors went snip, snap, snip, and his needle went in and out and in and out, "there's just enough material here to make…" a wonderful tie. Joseph wore the wonderful tie to his grandparent's house every Friday.

Joseph loved his wonderful tie and wore to synagogue every week. But as Joseph grew older, the wonderful tie grew older, too.

One day his mother said to him, "Joseph, look at your tie! It's stained with soup, it's torn and tattered, and the end droops. It is time to throw it out!"

"But Mama, Grandpa can fix it," Joseph said. So Joseph took his tie to his granfather.

Grandfather took the tie and turned it round and round.

"Hmm," he said as his scissors went snip, snap, snip, and his needle went in and out and in and out, "there's just enough material here to make…" a wonderful handkerchief. Joseph used the wonderful hand-kerchief to keep his marbles safe.

Joseph loved his wonderful handkerchief and carried it in his pocket everyday. But as Joseph grew older, his wonderful handkerchief grew older, too.

One day his mother said to him, "Joseph, look at your handkerchief! It's been used till it's torn and tattered, it's splotched and splattered. It is time to THROW IT OUT!"

"But Mama, Grandpa can fix it," said Joseph. So Joseph took his handkerchief to his grandfather.

Grandfather took the handkerchief and turned it round and round.

"Hmm," he said as his scissors went snip, snap, snip, and his needle went in and out and in and out, "there's just enough material here to make..." a wonderful button. Joseph wore the wonderful button on his suspenders to hold his pants up everyday.

One day his mother said to him, "Joseph, where is your button?"

Joseph looked. It was gone!

He searched high and low, inside and out; he searched everywhere, but he could not find it.

Joseph ran down to his grandfather's house.

"My button! My wonderful button is lost!"

His mother ran after him. "Joseph! Listen to me. The button is gone, finished, kaput. Even your grandfather can't make something from nothing."

Joseph's grandfather shook his head sadly. "I'm afraid that your mother is right," he said.

The next day while Joseph was at school, "Hmm," he said, as his pen went scritch, scratch, scritch over the paper. "There's just enough material here to make..." a wonderful story.[10]

Reflections on the Story

Humanity tends to be struck by the improbability of accomplishing a promise, more than they are awed by the possibilities a promise offers. Like Abraham, we want to have hope; we want to believe that through God anything is possible. But, more often than not, our thoughts and actions betray our skepticism, and we laugh. A story for this text needs to focus on the possibility, in the face of opposition, of the improbable. "Something from Nothing" offers a story of hope in the possibility that something good can occur in the face of a reality which makes hope appear futile.

In "Something from Nothing" a cherished and beloved blanket becomes old and worn, to the point that it is no longer serviceable. This makes a nice parallel to Sarah. Society had judged, and unfortunately still does, a woman's "serviceability" by her ability to conceive and bear children. Sarah has not been able to conceive a child, and whether we believe she is ninety years old or not, is at least past the time of menstruation and is now considered old and worn. We hear the voice of Abraham in the mother who attempts to convince the boy that the blanket is beyond use, just as Abraham tried to convince God concerning Sarah. For the boy's part, he steadfastly believes in the hope that there is something from nothing in the worn and tattered blanket. And indeed, there is. The grandfather is able to make something from nothing: a jacket, a vest, a tie, a handkerchief, and a button. Even when the button is lost and all hope should be lost, something literally comes from nothing: a wonderful story. From nothing, the empty womb of Sarah, came something: a son, nations, kings, and land. For God nothing is impossible, and the improbable becomes the reality. So when we doubt and laugh at what God says will be done, it is always God who has the last laugh.

NOTES

[1] J. Gerald Janzen, *Abraham and All the Families of the Earth: A Commentary on the Book of Genesis 12–50* (Grand Rapids: William B. Eerdmans Publishing, 1993), p. 47; also see Michael Maher, *Genesis* (Wilmington, Delaware: Michael Glazier, 1982), p. 108, and John C. Holbert, *Genesis,* ed. Michael E. Williams (Nashville: Abingdon Press, 1991), p. 83.

[2] Janzen, *Abraham and All the Families of the Earth*, p. 50.

[3] Holbert, *Genesis*, p. 83; also see Maher, *Genesis*, p. 108.

[4] Holbert, *Genesis*, p. 83.

[5] Ibid.

[6] Ibid., p. 84.

[7] Maher, *Genesis*, p. 109.

[8] Ibid.; also see Holbert, *Genesis*, p. 84.

[9] Janzen, *Abraham and All the Families of the Earth*, p. 51f.

[10] A Jewish folktale.

7

Aunt Dicey's Funeral

Genesis 15:1–6   **Week 2 Of Lent, Year C**

After these things the word of the LORD came to Abram in a vision, "Do not be afraid, Abram, I am your shield; your reward shall be very great." But Abram said, "O Lord GOD, what will you give me, for I continue childless, and the heir of my house is Eliezer of Damascus?" And Abram said, "You have given me no offspring, and so a slave born in my house is to be my heir." But the word of the LORD came to him, "This man shall not be your heir; no one but your very own issue shall be your heir." He brought him outside and said, "Look toward heaven and count the stars, if you are able to count them." Then he said to him, "So shall your descendants be." And he believed the LORD; and the LORD reckoned it to him as righteousness.

Comments on the Text

One of the most persistent questions all Christians ask and have to deal with is, "Why do bad things happen to good people?" For a child who has had to face the death of a parent, the brutality of physical and/or sexual abuse, or even the crisis of a death of a beloved pet, this question is a reality that makes no sense. God has promised us a life full of abundance, yet we all must live that promised life in the midst of famine. The real question that we must ask ourselves, as Walter Brueggemann reminds us, is, "Why and how does one continue to trust solely in the promise when the evidence against the promise is all around?"[1] This is the question that "Father Abraham" faces head on and argues out with God.

Before beginning a study of this text, it is important to step back and review what has transpired just prior to this story. In chapter 12 Abram is described as a shameful liar who passes off his wife, Sarai, as his sister so that he will not be killed. Not only does Abram lie to the Egyptians about the identity of his wife; Abram accepts a king's ransom in payment from the Pharaoh so that Sarai will become a wife of the Pharaoh. In chapters 13 and 14 a different portrait of Abram is painted. Here Abram offers his nephew, Lot, first choice of land. Later Abram mounts a rescue raid to free Lot from a coalition of Eastern kings. In gratitude for helping defeat this coalition, Melchizedek of Salem offers Abram to "take the goods for yourself" (14:21). But Abram refuses to take any of the spoils of battle as he had promised YHWH. It is in this contradiction of character, of being greedy and selfish (12), and generous, brave, and honest (13–14), that we all gain hope. Like the patriarch of the faith, we too are imperfect and flawed.

As this text begins, we must remember that YHWH has previously made the promise of progeny and land to Abram, but the realization of this promise has yet to come to fruition. Abram and his band are still strangers in a foreign land. The land of promise, "all the land that you see" (13:15), is still inhabited and ruled by other kings. Abram and Sarai are still childless and not getting any younger. Not even one of the promised offspring that will number as many as "the dust of the earth" (13:16) has been born. YHWH's promises appear to be as barren as Sarai's womb. So it is that after all the promises made, the lies told, and the honesty shown, "after these things" (15:1) YHWH comes to Abram in a vision to discuss the promises.

The scene is one of sharp confrontation. Abram stands toe to toe with the deity, slugging it out by refuting both the promises and the reassurances offered by YHWH. This is not a scene of the faithful and obedient servant blindly accepting the offerings of the master. This is a scene of an angry man who wants to know what has happened to all the promises that were made to him. The scene can be looked at as a four-step process: YHWH's basic promise of land and progeny, "your reward shall be very great" (15:1); Abram's disillusionment with the promise, "what will you give me?" (15:2–3); YHWH's response to Abram's disillusionment, "your very own issue shall be your heir" (15:4–5); and Abram's acceptance of the promise maker, "he believed the Lord" (15:6).[2]

YHWH comes to Abram in a vision speaking typical theophany (God appearance) words of assurance, "Do not be afraid, Abram" (15:1). But the words of assurance offered by YHWH go beyond calming the mere mortal in the presence of the divine being. YHWH also reassures Abram that the promises, or "reward," made earlier by YHWH will indeed be "very great" and will come to be (15:1).[3] Abram's response to these words of assurance that the promises will be fulfilled is full of doubt and frustration. In frustration Abram chides YHWH because "you have given me no offspring" (15:3) to inherit the land. The only possible *human* way that Abram sees for the promises to be fulfilled is through the adoption of the slave Eliezer of Damascus. However, Abram complains that the human way of fulfillment is not what was promised.[4]

A *divine* way to fulfill the promises is needed so that a biological heir can be produced. The need for a biological heir is necessary for several reasons. Fulfilling the promise of progeny is obvious: Without offspring that comes from one's own "seed," there can be no descendants, let alone more descendants than the dust of the earth. Land ownership also depends on a biological heir. Possession of "land is never for one generation. The capacity to transmit land for long generations to come is required."[5] Abram's frustration with YHWH is that the one and only thing needed to fulfill the promises has not occurred. Abram's response questions whether YHWH will provide the divine way to fulfill the promise.

YHWH is undeterred by Abram's rejection of the promise. Taking Abram by the hand, YHWH leads him outside and asks Abram to "count the stars, if you are able to count them" (15:5). This action by YHWH serves as a sign for Abram, reminding him that YHWH is the God of creation. Just as YHWH created the heavens out of nothing, so too can YHWH create a nation out of the barrenness of Abram and Sarai.[6]

Unlike Abram's previous rejection of YHWH's words of assurance, Abram now accepts the words and sign of the promise. The narrator informs us that Abram "believed the LORD" (15:6). YHWH's promise is not dependent upon the belief of Abram. Abram lacks belief in the promise; it is not until he has faith in the promise-maker that he has belief in the promise.

The hardship and pain that many suffer in life makes it nearly impossible to believe in the promises of an abundant life. However, when we can move beyond the promises to the promise-maker, true belief in the promises becomes a reality. The promises of God often seem just as impossible and ludicrous to us as the promise of offspring was to Abram. But like Abram, we also can see the signs of the promise if we will only look.

Aunt Dicey's Funeral

Back in the days when white people owned black people, life for the slaves was very hard. They had no rights; they couldn't do what they wanted to do; they couldn't go where they wanted. Sometimes mamas and daddies where sold to different folks, and even children were taken from their mamas when they were just babies and sold to other white people far away. And them mamas would never see their babies ever again. Black people didn't have any choice; they had to do whatever white people told them to do. Life was very hard and sad.

But no matter how hard it got, no matter how sad it was, the slaves always helped each other. Nobody was ever left to suffer alone. When a black person was sick, a black man or woman who had the healing touch would make some tea or a poultice to help the sick person get well. And others would cook the meals, wash the clothes, and look after the children. And all this love would always make the sufferer feel better inside, whether they got well or died.

Now there was one such woman, named Aunt Dicey. Aunt Dicey looked after everybody, white or black. She was so full of love that everybody loved and respected her. One late evenin' Aunt Dicey passed away in her sleep nice and peaceful like.

You remember how I told you that the slaves always looked after each other in those days? Well, slaves didn't have undertakers or funeral directors, so the womenfolk came in and prepared Aunt Dicey for burial. They washed her from top to bottom, dressed her in the best dress they could find, and gently laid her in a homemade coffin that some of the men had made out of the best scraps of lumber they could find. When they had finished, ol' Aunt Dicey looked as peaceful as any angel in heaven.

Now in the evening the slaves would come to the home of the dead person to pay their last respects. And folks came to Aunt Dicey's all night long. They would sing and pray and sing some more. Most of the songs they sang were sad songs with happy endings, because Aunt Dicey was now free from all the sadness and pain of slavery and was now safe in heaven, free at last. Aunt Dicey wasn't a poor, barefoot slave dressed in rags anymore; now she was in heaven where she'd have everything she needed to make her happy. And so they sang some more.

Just thinking about heaven kept the mourners from being too sad about Aunt Dicey's going away. Because they knew she was better off with a loving heavenly father than she had ever been in this wicked world of slavery. Then they'd get all happy again and sing some more. All night long they sang and prayed and sang some more.

In the morning they loaded up the coffin with Aunt Dicey into master John Brown's best farm wagon drawn by two good mules. Master Brown let the slaves use the wagon and mules because even he loved and respected Aunt Dicey. One by one the slaves followed the wagon out to the slaves' graveyard. The line of mourners was so long that some said the line stretched out for more than a mile.

After Aunt Dicey was laid in the grave, the slave preacher said some words of comfort. He said something like this: "Sister Dicey, you are now in the arms of God. Taken out of the misery of this world. I commit your body to the ground, earth to earth, ashes to ashes, dust to dust, where it will rest in peace. But on that Great Getting-Up Morning, when God blows that trumpet and wakes up all the dead, we will all meet you again as we join the host of saints who will go marching in. Yes, we want to be in that number, Miz Dicey, when the saints go marching in."

Now, before the preacher could even finish, some folks got so happy that they drowned him out with their singing and clapping and shouting, just thinking about God's promise. After the grave had been filled up properly with dirt, some folks laid flowers and ribbons on the grave. And a man put an old broken shingle at the head of the grave to mark the spot where Aunt Dicey laid. The shingle didn't have no words on it, though, because slaves could not read or write. But that didn't matter none because no one could own their souls or keep them from loving each other. Those things come only from God.[7]

Reflections on the Story

No other circumstance or condition can set the stage of doubting the promises of God better than slavery does. Slavery is the total denial of God's promises. Slaves lived in a land of barrenness and had every right to live in a state of hopelessness in the face of God's promise. But here in the story of "Aunt Dicey's Funeral" we see the faith of those who have put their trust not in the promises, but in the promise-maker. In despair and misfortune, the slaves where able to look beyond their current circumstance and really see God, and believe that God's freedom was not a shallow promise, but a covenant pledged in love.

NOTES

[1] Walter Brueggemann, *Genesis* (Atlanta: John Knox Press, 1982), p. 140.

[2] Ibid.

[3] John Holbert, *Genesis,* ed. Michael E. Williams (Nashville: Abingdon Press, 1991), p. 74.

[4] Ibid.; also see Terence E. Fretheim, "The Book of Genesis," *The New Interpreter's Bible,* vol. 1 (Nashville: Abingdon Press, 1995), p. 445.

[5] Fretheim, "The Book of Genesis," p. 445.

[6] Brueggemann, *Genesis*, p. 144.

[7] An African-American slave-era tale.

8

The Smuggler

John 3:11–21

"Very truly, I tell you, we speak of what we know and testify to what we have seen; yet you do not receive our testimony. If I have told you about earthly things and you do not believe, how can you believe if I tell you about heavenly things? No one has ascended into heaven except the one who descended from heaven, the Son of Man. And just as Moses lifted up the serpent in the wilderness, so must the Son of Man be lifted up, that whoever believes in him may have eternal life.

"For God so loved the world that he gave his only Son, so that everyone who believes in him may not perish but may have eternal life.

"Indeed, God did not send the Son into the world to condemn the world, but in order that the world might be saved through him. Those who believe in him are not condemned; but those who do not believe are condemned already, because they have not believed in the name of the only Son of God. And this is the judgment, that the light has come into the world, and people loved darkness rather than light because their deeds were evil. For all who do evil hate the light and do not come to the light, so that their deeds may not be exposed. But those who do what is true come to the light, so that it may be clearly seen that their deeds have been done in God."

Comments on the Text

There is an old saying that goes "Do not believe it until you have seen it." Miracles tend to have this same effect on people. Because some witness a miraculous event, they are transformed and have faith. However, in a great many of these cases it is not God that they have new faith in but faith in the miracle itself. Miracles and signs affect the intellect but have no effect on the heart and soul. For faith to be complete, faith must include the heart, mind, and soul. The Nicodemus story displays God's call for a transformation that can only come from a complete and total faith.

This lectionary text is Jesus' monologue section of the Nicodemus story that begins at John 2:23.[1] Although Nicodemus is not present in this selected pericope, it is important for our understanding to move back and examine Nicodemus' role in the total story before moving to the actual text at hand. First, we need to recognize that "signs" (the word used in the Gospel of John for miracles) are a signal to the reader. Signs point beyond themselves to the glory of Jesus, or in other words, point to who Jesus is. Therefore, to see beyond the signs of Jesus is to understand who Jesus is. In the dialogue between Jesus and Nicodemus, Nicodemus claims to believe in the signs that Jesus has done, but he cannot see beyond the miracles themselves (3:2). As Raymond Brown suggests, "For John, failure to believe fully is to be traced to the unwillingness of the hearers, not to any secrets on Jesus' part."[2]

Nicodemus should not be viewed as a particular character, but as a representative character. He is best understood as a stereotype of any and all people who have inadequate faith.[3] Nicodemus is an example of the "many" who "believed in his name because they saw the signs that he was doing," but whom Jesus "would not entrust himself to" (2:23–24). Nicodemus' inadequate faith is further underscored by the use of darkness (a frequent metaphorical symbol in John). Nicodemus comes to Jesus "by night" (3:2). Whether Nicodemus literally comes in darkness or not is not important. Symbolically, Nicodemus is in the dark about who Jesus is, as well as being separated from the presence of God.[4] The dark is the place where one is blind and cannot see what is right in front of her or him. This understanding of the darkness is further enhanced by verse 19, the "people loved darkness rather than light because their deeds were evil." As the drama unfolds, Nicodemus moves back into the shadows or darkness (3:10) and is not seen again, presumably because he is one who "loved the darkness rather than light."

Nicodemus demonstrates his inadequate faith by his lack of understanding Jesus' statement concerning being "born from above" or "born again" (3:3). The Greek word used here has a double meaning that no one English word or phrase can duplicate. The Johannine community, however, would immediately understand this double meaning. They would recognize at once that it can mean to be born "from above" or born "again." The community knows that Jesus means "born from above" and understands the spiritual nature of Jesus' statement.[5] The question, because of its double meaning, reminds the hearers that Jesus is from above, "born, not of blood or of the will of the flesh or of the will of humanity, but of God" (1:13). Jesus' answer to Nicodemus' initial question is meant to inform those with inadequate faith that Jesus did not come from God in the sense of a prophet being approved by God. But Jesus is from God in a new sense, as one who is descended from God's presence to lift people up to God. Nicodemus and the "many" he represents, because they have faith only in the signs and not in what the signs point to, become stuck on the biological function of the meaning of the word and cannot comprehend Jesus and his rather obscure explanation. Nicodemus is a character representing inadequate faith, and a person of inadequate faith will not be able to understand because they come to faith "by night" (3:2), and choose to remain in the dark unable to "come to the light" (3:20). Nicodemus does not understand Jesus' obtuse answer and requests further explanation. Misunderstandings are a frequent literary tool used by the Johannine author to allow Jesus to explain more fully the meaning of his words. Jesus again answers Nicodemus in such a way that even the hearers of the story scratch their heads in wonder. So it is no surprise that Nicodemus again asks Jesus to explain this physical impossibility by saying, "How can this be?" In a dramatic visual representation of the story, Nicodemus fades back into the dark night from which he came. This is done to demonstrate that those who have faith only in the signs and cannot see what lies beyond them remain both physically and spiritually in the dark with their inadequate faith.[6]

Jesus begins a long monologue at verse 11. Here in verse 11 there is a sudden shift as to who Jesus is addressing. Jesus is no longer speaking directly to Nicodemus or to those whom Nicodemus represents. The author now has Jesus addressing the community of believers. This is accomplished by the author's shift from using the pronoun "you," which is commonly used to address Jesus' detractors, to the plural pronoun "we," used by the author to distinguish the Johannine community. Here in verse 11 the author moves away from the "historical/mythological" story line of Nicodemus, to address the experiences of the community to which the Gospel was initially addressed. "We speak of what we know and testify to what we have seen; yet you do not receive our testimony" (3:11).

The Johannine community, it must be remembered, was a community that worshiped and practiced as Jesus did and considered themselves Jewish in all respects. The synagogue was the center of their religious activities, but by the time of, or shortly before, the Gospel's writing, the community was being excluded and expelled from the synagogue (9:34). In some cases those who confessed Jesus as the Messiah (9:22) were facing violence from those who were at one time their brothers and sisters of the faith. This crisis of faith had to be made comprehensible. Beginning in verse 11 the community is able to take to heart the story of Jesus and make it their own. They are able to find self-identification and hope for their present condition. They have been faithful witnesses, yet others within the same original faith community have not received the testimony.

Adequate or true faith is not found in the signs, but in what the signs point to: Jesus, "the Son of Man" (3:13), the "only Son" (3:16) of God. It is only through being "born again" or being "born from above" that one can truly "see" the signs and come to the light of true faith. Verses 16–21 are the rationale for having true faith or why one should "come to the light."[7] The rationale is more clearly seen in verses 16–18. If one has proper faith they will receive eternal life (3:16), the world will be saved (3:17), and those who believe in the Son of Man will not be condemned (3:18). Verses 19–21 are like verse 11; they are an explanation and a point in the story in which the Johannine community is incorporated, so that they feel that the story of Nicodemus is their story. Some in the original faith community have not accepted the "testimony" but have chosen instead to remain in the "darkness rather than light because their deeds were evil" (3:19). The deeds of darkness, no doubt, refers to the expulsions and violence that the community suffered from some people in the original faith community.[8] The message is clear to this community that is experiencing anxiety over being separated from the synagogue: There is no salvation apart from Jesus. In Jesus, God presented the world with a decision. Jesus was sent by God into the world in order to save it, but each person must decide on his or her own to accept the offer of salvation. It is this decision that separates good and evil, light and dark.

The light illuminates, so that the believer is able to see more clearly and perceive what is to be "done in God" (3:21). It is not just the intellectual and spiritual side that must come to the light; the physical side of the person of faith must also come to the light. The actions and deeds of the believer are also part of true faith. Only speaking the words and going through the religious motions of faith is inadequate faith; true faith is putting the words of faith into action. As Dennis E. Smith says, "The Nicodemuses of the world might be able to say all the right things, but until they put their lives on the line for the faith, they are still people who 'prefer darkness to light.'"[9] True faith is a transforming event. It transforms our minds, our hearts, and our souls so that even our deeds reflect who we believe in and where we stand.

CHILDREN'S SERMON ━━━━━━━━━━━━━━━━━

The Smuggler

There once was a clever border inspector. He was so good at his job that he caught everyone who ever tried to smuggle goods into the country. Some said the inspector could smell a smuggler a mile away. And so it happened one day that a smuggler led a donkey loaded with bundles of straw to the border. The inspector eyed the donkey's bundles with suspicion.

"You must allow me to search your bundles!" the inspector insisted. "I know that you are a smuggler and have hidden a valuable treasure on the donkey that you wish to sell at the market. And when I find it, you must pay me a border fee."

"Search if you will," said the smuggler. "If you find something other than straw, I will gladly pay whatever fee you ask."

The inspector pulled apart the straw bundles until there was straw here, straw there, straw everywhere. Yet the inspector could find nothing.

"You are a clever smuggler!" said the inspector. "I know that you are hiding something. What it is I do not know. Now be gone. Go!"

The smuggler crossed the border with his donkey. And all the suspicious inspector could do was look on with a scowl.

The next day the smuggler returned to the border with a donkey again loaded with straw. Once again the inspector pulled apart the bundles. There was straw here, straw there, straw everywhere.

"Not one valuable thing have I found!" the exasperated inspector said. "Go!" he shouted at the smuggler. Again the smuggler and the donkey went across the border. "Bah!" cried the inspector once again, scowling.

This happened again the next day and the next day. Every day for ten long years, the smuggler came to the border with a donkey loaded with straw. And each day the inspector carefully searched the straw, but he found nothing.

Finally, the inspector retired. Even as an old man, he could not stop thinking about that smuggler. One day as he was walking through the marketplace, still trying to solve the mystery, he muttered to himself, "I know that man was smuggling something. Perhaps I should have looked more carefully in the donkey's mouth. He could have hidden something between the hairs on the donkey's tail!"

As he mumbled to himself, he noticed a familiar face in the crowd. "You!" he exclaimed. "I know you! You are the smuggler who came to the border every day with a donkey loaded with straw. Come and speak with me!"

The smuggler walked toward him, and the old inspector said, "Admit it! You were smuggling goods across the border, weren't you?"

The smuggler nodded and grinned.

"Aha!" said the old inspector. "Just as I suspected. You were sneaking something to the market! Was it silver or gold?"

"No," the smuggler answered.

"Was it emeralds or rubies?" questioned the inspector.

"No," the smuggler replied.

"Tell me what it was! What were you smuggling? Tell me, if you can," implored the confused inspector.

"Donkeys," said the smuggler.[10]

Reflections on the Story

The Nicodemus story has many levels and many points of consideration. Like the community of the Johannine author, we, too, can identify with the story. More often than not, we identify with Nicodemus. Like Nicodemus, we are in the dark most of the time, stumbling and struggling to know what is right and what is wrong, what to do and what not to do. To come to the light and have the adequate faith that the author of John describes, we, too, must look deeper and far beyond what we see on the surface. As my mother always told me, "It's what is on the inside that counts."

The story of the smuggler is a story that reminds people to look beyond what we think we are seeing. The inspector, perceiving the man to be a smuggler, naturally assumed he would hide the smuggled goods somewhere on the donkey. The inspector became stuck on what he thought was the logical conclusion of being a smuggler, just as Nicodemus becomes stuck on the biological understanding of being "born again." Because the inspector could not see beyond the typical smuggled goods (jewels, gold, and silver), he never saw what was really there right in front of his face, the donkey. Nicodemus could not see who Jesus really was either, although he was face to face with the reality.

NOTES

[1] There is a great deal of debate as to the beginning point of this story. Many contend that the Nicodemus story begins at verse 1, and that 2:23–25 is only a bridge between the temple story and the Nicodemus story. Dennis E. Smith, however, makes a convincing argument for the inclusion of these verses within the Nicodemus story. See Dennis E. Smith, *John*, ed. Dennis E. Smith and Michael E. Williams (Nashville: Abingdon Press, 1996), p. 52.

[2] Raymond E. Brown, *The Gospel According to John I–XIII*, vol. 1 (New York: Doubleday, 1966), p. 127.

[3] Smith, *John*, p. 52; also see Ernst Haenchen, *John 1: A Commentary on the Gospel of John Chapters 1–6*, translated by Robert W. Funk (Philadelphia: Fortress Press, 1984), p. 199.

[4] Gail R. O' Day, "The Gospel of John," *The New Interpreter's Bible*, vol. 9 (Nashville: Abingdon Press, 1995), p. 548.

[5] Ibid., p. 200; also see O' Day, "The Gospel of John, p. 549.

[6] Smith, *John*, p. 53; also see Brown, *The Gospel According to John*, p. 145.

[7] Brown, *The Gospel According to John*, p. 147.

[8] Smith, *John*, p. 54.

[9] Ibid.

[10] A Middle Eastern folktale.

9

The Tiger's Whisker

Jeremiah 31:31–34   **Week 5 of Lent, Year B**

The days are surely coming, says the LORD, when I will make a new covenant with the house of Israel and the house of Judah. It will not be like the covenant that I made with their ancestors when I took them by the hand to bring them out of the land of Egypt—a covenant that they broke, though I was their husband, says the LORD. But this is the covenant that I will make with the house of Israel after those days, says the LORD: I will put my law within them, and I will write it on their hearts; and I will be their God, and they shall be my people. No longer shall they teach one another, or say to each other, "Know the LORD," for they shall all know me, from the least of them to the greatest, says the LORD; for I will forgive their iniquity, and remember their sin no more.

Comments on the Text

One of the most difficult things in the world is to get a congregation to change. Even the smallest change, such as the placement of floral arrangements in the sanctuary, can cause a congregation-wide uproar. Change in religious circles has never been easy. "We have always done it that way" may be the most universal phrase among religious participants in all world religions and Christian denominations. This Jeremiah passage had to have

76

been one of the most shocking passages heard in Palestine when it was first written. God is instituting a major change within the theological precepts of the people, a change with far more implications than where the flowers should be placed.

There is considerable debate among scholars as to whether this oracle of hope can actually be attributed to the historical prophet Jeremiah or if it is an editorial redaction.[1] Whichever may be the case, this oracle causes people to look again at their relationship with God, and their relationships with others in the faith community. To fully appreciate and understand why a change in the people's relationship with God and with each other was needed, we must remember what was happening at the time of Jeremiah's writings. Jerusalem had fallen to the Babylonians, and the temple had been destroyed. The Judean political and religious hierarchy was sent into exile in far-off Babylon, leaving the mass population leaderless, both politically and religiously. The people were left wondering where God was and why God had abandoned them. The Jewish people were lost and confused, believing that the "everlasting covenant" between God and the descendants of Abraham (the land promised in perpetuity to Abraham and his decendants in Gen. 17:4–8), had been broken by God. Because of the radical socio-political changes occurring all around the people, a change in the religious theology of the people was required to answer the question "Where is God, and why would God abandon God's chosen people, in effect breaking the 'everlasting covenant'?" (Gen. 17:7) The answer to this question is found in a covenant that is written "on their hearts" (31:33).

Before proceeding further it should be noted that this passage, like several other Old Testament passages, most notably the servant songs of Isaiah, have been preempted by many Christians, "as though Jews belong to the old covenant now nullified and Christians are the sole heirs of the new covenant."[2] This type of interpretation ignores the content and context of the text. The oracle should not be read as the foreshadowing of the New Testament. Rather, it should be read as humanity's further development in understanding humanity's relationship with God and with each other, and as the restoration of the Israelite community.

In verse 31 the prophet begins by addressing the people of both conquered kingdoms. "The house of Israel" is used to denote the Northern Kingdom and "the house of Judah" the Southern Kingdom. The new covenant is not just for the people of the South but is for all of God's people. In verse 32 the prophet answers the question "Why has God broken the everlasting covenant?" The answer is startling: It is not God who has broken the covenant, but it is "a covenant that they [the people] broke...I [YHWH] was their husband" (31:32).[3]

The reference to the exodus, "out of the land of Egypt" (31:32), reminds the reader that the old covenant was written on "stone" and given to the people at Sinai. From its very beginning, the "old covenant" was a covenant that the people resisted; recall the golden calf incident when Moses did not come down from Mount Sinai quickly enough for the Israelites (Ex. 32:1–29). But now a new covenant will be made, one in which YHWH's law will be put "within them" (31:33). As Walter Brueggemann concludes:

> The new covenant will not be resisted, because the torah—the same commandments as at Sinai—will be written on their hearts. That is, the commandments will not be an external rule which invites hostility, but now will be embraced, an internal identity-giving mark, so that obeying will be as normal and as readily accepted as breathing and eating.[4]

The law of Moses, or Torah, under the new covenant has not changed, but how people will receive the law has. Instead of being an external rod of punishment, God will transform the law so that when it is received by those with an inclined heart it will be natural and normal for people to act in accord with the law.

Through this transformation, the fruits of the covenant will be realized: "I will be their God, and they shall be my people" (31:33). This covenantal formula is found in similar statements throughout the Old Testament. However, it is a stark reminder that God desires, above all else, to be in relationship with humanity. This idea is further magnified when YHWH declares that in the new covenant "they shall all know me, from the least of them to the greatest" (31:34). "To know the Lord" was the concept of teaching the identity-giving, or traditional, stories. It is also "probable that 'knowledge of Yahweh' means affirmation of Yahweh as sovereign Lord with readiness to obey the commands for justice that are the will of Yahweh."[5] The most likely meaning of "to know the Lord" in the new covenant that God establishes is a combination of the two. Thus, in the new covenant a personal relationship with God and a communal relationship with God are created through the sharing of tradition stories.

The final change involved in the new covenant is the openness to whom it is given. It is not yet a universal covenant open to both Gentiles and Jews, although it could be argued that the beginnings of a universal God are starting to emerge. The openness to God is found in the egalitarian statement "from the least of them to the greatest" (31:34). Access to God is now open to all classes and, I would argue, all genders, although history proves that gender equality was not achieved. "No one has superior, elitist access, and no one lacks what is required. All share fully in the new relations."[6] This is an important point. The elite no longer have exclusive control over the access to God. Keep in mind that the elite and powerful have been exiled. The door to God is now open to all people; young and old, rich and poor.

There are good changes and bad. Whichever it may be, change is inevitable. Jeremiah reminds us that the world around us will change, causing us at times to feel abandoned and alone. Yet, we are not alone. God is with us through it all, and God is willing to change the rules so that we can always be in relationship with God and each other.

CHILDREN'S SERMON ━━━━━━━━━━━━━━━━━━━━

The Tiger's Whisker

After many years away from home at war, a fierce warrior was finally able to return home. The warrior had spent so many years at war there was no longer any love in his heart. He was so somber that his wife thought his spirit had been killed in battle, and only flesh and bones had walked through the door. Although she welcomed him with great embraces and tears of joy, he did not respond to her touch. His icy eyes did not meet her gaze. He seated himself at the table and stared out the window.

The wife tried to engage him in conversation, but he did not reply. She prepared huge, tasty meals, which he barely ate. She told him jokes and the news of things he had missed while he was away. But no matter what she did, the warrior remained quiet and sullen.

The wife became upset at his coldness. She scolded him for being cruel and hardhearted. "How can you treat me this way?" she wailed. "I have waited so long for your return and suffered in my loneliness!" She dashed out the door and ran until she came to the house of a wise old man who was known to make potions and magical charms.

Tearfully, she pleaded with the old man, "Please sir, give me a love potion that will make my husband love me again."

The old man listened carefully to her complaint and finally replied, "I can help you win back your husband's love, but to make the potion, I will need the whisker of a tiger. If you can bring me a tiger's whisker, I can help you win back your husband's love."

The woman's mouth dropped open, and her eyebrows arched in surprise. "A tiger's whisker!" she exclaimed. "How will I get a tiger's whisker? It is impossible!"

The old man replied, "If you truly want to win the love of your husband, then you will bring me what I ask."

The woman walked away from the old man's house, deep in thought. Her heart ached. She could not bear the situation as it was, so she decided to go to the market and buy a piece of meat.

Carrying the meat, she went into the jungle until she saw the cave of a tiger. Hiding at a distance, she saw that the huge cat was sleeping in the sun. The woman immediately noticed its sharp claws and long teeth. She sat as still as a stone and watched. At last, she left the meat on the spot where she had been sitting and went home.

Every day after that, the woman returned to the tiger's cave with meat. Each day, she left the meat a few inches closer and patiently watched the animal. After several weeks, the tiger allowed her to approach and place the meat in front of him. Eventually, the tiger allowed her to sit beside him as he ate. He would then stretch himself and sleep with his head near her lap. The first time she reached out and stroked his fur, the tiger began to purr like a giant house cat.

Many days later, as she sat beside the tiger, she took a tiny pair of scissors from her pocket and carefully snipped a whisker.

Once she was out of the jungle, the woman ran all the way to the old man's house. Clutching the tiger's whisker, she shouted, "Here it is! I have the tiger's whisker! Please, make me the love potion that will win back my husband's love."

The old man took the whisker and examined it carefully. "It is truly what you say it is. Tell me, how did you get it?"

The woman replied, "I was very patient. I approached the tiger carefully and gently, leaving my offerings at a great distance. Each day, I came just a bit closer. After a long time, when I was certain that the tiger trusted me, I moved closer. Finally, I was able to reach out and touch him, because he was not afraid of me."

"That is very interesting," the old man said, as he tossed the whisker into the fire.

The woman shrieked with alarm. "After all my effort you have thrown away the special ingredient you needed to make my love potion!"

The old man smiled gently and replied, "You do not need a love potion. Any woman who can tame a tiger can just as easily win the love of her husband. Go home, dear woman, and be patient with your husband. Trust that the magic charm to win his heart is already within you."

The woman returned home with new understanding. She stopped scolding. She stopped demanding love. With the same great patience and the gentle warmth that had tamed the tiger, she melted the icy heart of her warrior husband.[7]

Reflections on the Story

Human nature is such that we have a tendency to long for what was. We nostalgically remember when things were better, easier, and more fulfilling. It was a time before "the event" changed everything. In most cases those times were not really any better, easier, or more fulfilling, but we understood our place in the world during that time. Jeremiah reminds us that no matter how unsettling change may be, we can get through it, and in the end we can be stronger than we were before. "The Tiger's Whisker" is a story that offers young people a way to understand that through love, patience, and kindness we can cope with all manner of change.

The warrior husband, like Israel and Judah, has witnessed years of war and deprivation. The war has changed him. The warrior's heart is hardened, and he is no longer the loving husband the wife remembers. Understandably, the wife wants her husband to be the same man he was before the war, but the war will not release him. Because of her quest for a tiger's whisker she discovers that the only way to rebuild a relationship with her husband is through love, patience, and kindness. A relationship cannot be forced or nagged into existence. True relationship comes when people are willing to be patient, loving, and kind to each other. Unfortunately, just like the people of Judah and Israel, at times we also become hardhearted and begin to question and distrust God. But God chooses to use love, patience, and kindness by writing God's covenant on a warm heart instead of a cold stone.

NOTES

[1] William L. Holladay, *Jeremiah 2: A Commentary on the Book of the Prophet Jeremiah*, vol. 2 (Minneapolis: Fortress Press, 1989), p. 197. Also see Walter Brueggemann, *To Build, To Plant: A Commentary on Jeremiah 26—52* (Grand Rapids: William B. Eerdmans Publishing, 1991), p. 69, and R. E. Clements, *Jeremiah* (Atlanta: John Knox Press, 1988), p. 190.

[2] Brueggemann, *To Build, To Plant*, p. 69.

[3] Holladay, *Jeremiah 2*, p. 198.

[4] Brueggemann, *To Build, To Plant*, p. 71.

[5] Ibid.

[6] Ibid., p. 72; also see Holladay, *Jeremiah 2*, p. 199.

[7] A Korean folktale.

10

Czar Trojan's Ears

Mark 16:1–8   **Easter Sunday, Year B**

When the sabbath was over, Mary Magdalene, and Mary the mother of James, and Salome bought spices, so that hey might go and anoint him. And very early on the first day of the week, when the sun had risen, they went to the tomb. They had been saying to one another, "Who will roll away the stone for us from the entrance to the tomb?" When they looked up, they saw that the stone, which was very large, had already been rolled back. As they entered the tomb, they saw a young man, dressed in a white robe, sitting on the right side; and they were alarmed. But he said to them, "Do not be alarmed; you are looking for Jesus of Nazareth, who was crucified. He has been raised; he is not here. Look, there is the place they laid him. But go, tell his disciples and Peter that he is going ahead of you to Galilee; there you will see him, just as he told you." So they went out and fled from the tomb, for terror and amazement had seized them; and they said nothing to anyone, for they were afraid.

Comments on the Text

Testimony is one of the scariest words in the Christian language, especially among members of mainline denominations. So many negative connotations have been associated with the word that the idea of testifying about Jesus is horrifying. Yet, no matter how much we may want to deny the necessity of testimony, as Christians we are called "to testify because you have been with me from the beginning" (John 15:27). Humanity can often find comfort, strength, and courage when we learn that our heroes have fallen and tripped over the same obstacles that we have. The Mark account of the empty tomb reminds us that, like the disciples who were absent and the women who "said nothing," no matter how many times our faith is inadequate and no matter how many times we should have testified about the good news of Jesus Christ but remained silent, we can always return to God.

The predictions of death (8:31; 9:31; 10:34) and Jesus' own promise to "go before you [the disciples] to Galilee" (14:28), have led the hearers of the Gospel to believe that the story cannot end with the death and burial of Jesus. But in what is commonly called the first ending of Mark, this is exactly how the story ends. The story ends in mid-sentence: Jesus does not appear in glory to anyone, he does not meet the disciples in Galilee as promised, and most disturbing, the only people who know anything about what has happened to the body of Jesus flee in terror and never say anything to anyone.

How can the story end this way? How did the gospel message spread if no one said anything? The sudden and apparent incomplete ending to the Gospel caused early Christians to add either the short two-sentence ending usually found in the footnotes of most English translations of the Bible or the longer ending (16:9–20).[1] There is little scholarly debate and general agreement that neither of these two endings is authentic Mark. It is almost universally accepted that both endings are editorial redactions to give the Gospel a more complete ending. There is, however, considerable debate as to whether the "real" ending of Mark is lost, or if the author intentionally left the ending incomplete. As we examine the story in detail we will discover that the ending was not lost. The Gospel ends as it is written by the author because the story does not end with the appearance of Jesus to the disciples or with the ascension of Jesus. Each individual hearer of the Gospel must write her or his own ending by actions and responses to the good news. As Lamar Williamson, Jr., says, "No ending proposed by our decisions can contain him [Jesus], any more than the tomb with its great stone could. Always he goes before us; always he beckons forward to a new appearance in the Galilee of the nations, in the Galilee of our daily lives."[2]

The story contains three scenes. In the first scene the women are going to the tomb of Jesus to complete the burial preparations that they were not able to do before the Sabbath began Friday evening. The second scene is set in the tomb itself, where the women are given a message. In the final scene the women flee the tomb in fear. The three women listed as witnesses to the empty tomb are virtually identical to the list of women present at the death (15:40) and burial (15:47). The continual listing may appear redundant, but it makes the point that the same women were witnesses to the death, burial, and resurrection of Jesus. There are also two time designations contained in this opening scene: "When the sabbath was over" (16:1) and "very early on the first day of the week" (16:2). The hearers of this story are immediately reminded that Jesus' "third day" of resurrection (9:31 and 10:34) has come. As the women walk toward the tomb, they become concerned about "who will roll away the stone" (16:3) they witnessed Joseph of Arimathea place "against the door of the tomb" (15:46) when Jesus was buried three days previously. We are told that the stone is "very large," indicating that the women would need assistance to remove it. But as the women approach the tomb, to their amazement they discover that the stone has "already been rolled back" (16:4). In this state of uncertainty and bewilderment the three women enter the tomb.

When the women enter the tomb they are alarmed to find a "young man, dressed in a white robe" (16:5). There are a few scholars who contend this individual should be interpreted only as a young man. However, the scene should be interpreted as an angelophany, or an angel appearance. An angel is nothing other than a messenger, and the message that the "young man" brings is the heart of the good news: "He has been raised, he is not here" (16:6). The tomb is empty, the one they sought is gone. In all other angelophanies recorded in the Bible, it is necessary for the messenger to offer words to reassure and calm, just as the "young man" does in verse 6. But unlike the other angelophanies, the words of comfort and assurance offered by the messenger do nothing to relieve the fears of the women. Their fears are such that they are unable to complete the mission the messenger charges them with. The women are to tell the "disciples and Peter" that Jesus "is going ahead of you to Galilee; there you will see him, just as he told you" (16:7). But instead of telling the disciples "they said nothing to anyone, for they were afraid"(16:8).

In a traditional angelophany the women would have been reassured and their mission completed. But not in this story. The women remain silent and are even more frightened than they were before the words of assurance were offered. The reaction of the women is shocking to the hearers. Throughout the Gospel, it has been the women who faithfully "follow him and provided for him" (15:41). Unlike the disciples who have stumbled and fallen throughout the Gospel, the women have served steadfastly, always doing the right thing. But now in the final sentence of the Gospel they, too, flee, and in effect deny Jesus just as the men had done earlier. The one group of people the hearers have come to depend on to do the right thing have failed. The hearers know, because of clues left throughout the Gospel, that the crucifixion will not be the end of the story. The clues have led the hearers to believe that the reappearance of Jesus will be the climatic conclusion to the story. However, because the women tell no one about the resurrection, we are left hanging.

The end is not an end at all. Each individual hearer of the Gospel must bring the story to its conclusion; for each hearer must decide for themselves how they will react to the angel's message. Will they choose to tell others, or will they choose to remain silent? Whichever choice is made, the message of the angel to the disciples gives us all hope. In the message we discover grace for our own silence, the same grace given to the disciples and the women. The hearers of the story still remember that the disciples scattered immediately after Jesus' arrest and are not seen again in the Gospel, except for Peter. Peter's reappearance in the Gospel, however, is to deny Jesus (14:68, 70, and 71). The memory of Peter's denials still rings harshly in the hearer's ears. But now we are told that the disciples, and especially Peter, have been forgiven and are being called anew to Galilee, where a fresh start can begin, with Jesus going before them. Despite our failures, God continues to call us back to Galilee, where we, too, can begin again, with the good news going on before us.

CHILDREN'S SERMON ━━━━━━━━━━━━━━━━━━━━━━━━━━━

Czar Trojan's Ears

Once upon a time there lived a czar named Trojan. Trojan had the ears of a goat. The czar was very ashamed of his ears and did not want anyone to know. To hide his ears, the czar wore a great crown on his head all day and all night so that no one would ever find out about his sceret. The only time the czar took off his crown was to be shaved.

So each day he would call a barber to shave him, but none ever returned from the palace. After the barber had shaved the czar, he would ask him, "What do you see, my good man?" And the barber would answer, "I see that the czar has the ears of a goat." When the czar heard the barber's answer, he would order the barber's head to be chopped off at once.

One day the turn fell to a barber who was so frightened that he pretended to be ill. But in his place he sent his young apprentice.

While shaving the czar, the apprentice noticed that Trojan had the ears of a goat, but when the czar asked him what he saw, the apprentice answered, "I see nothing, Sire."

Trojan was so pleased that he gave the apprentice twelve gold coins and ordered him to come everyday to the palace to shave him.

When the apprentice returned home, the barber was curious and asked him about Czar Trojan. The apprentice told the barber that the czar was courteous and kind and had ordered him to come personally every day to shave the ruler. He then showed the barber the twelve gold coins, but he never said anything about the czar having the ears of a goat.

From that time on the apprentice went every day to shave the czar, and every day he received twelve gold coins. He never told a living soul the czar's secret. But after many months the apprentice began to worry and fret. The burden of carrying the czar's secret was growing heavier and heavier on his heart. He grew thinner and thinner, and sadder and sadder.

The barber noticed the change in his good-natured student, and asked what was troubling the boy.

"If only I could tell my secret to someone, my heart would be lightened," said the troubled apprentice.

The barber wanted to help, and he said, "Tell me, and I will tell no one; if you cannot tell me, then tell the priest; if you cannot tell him, then tell your dog."

"I cannot tell my secret to a living soul," wailed the apprentice.

"If you cannot tell me, or the priest, or your dog, then go out into the fields behind the town. Dig a hole. Put your head into it, and shout three times into the hole your secret. Then close the hole and come away."

The apprentice decided to tell his secret to the earth. He went out of town, dug a hole, put his head into it, and shouted three times, "Czar Trojan has the ears of a goat! Czar Trojan has the ears of goat! Czar Trojan has the ears of a goat!"

Covering the hole, he returned home, happy and contented for the first time in months.

In time, an elder tree grew on the spot where the apprentice had told his secret, and from the tree grew three branches as fine and straight as candles.

One day some shepherds found the elder tree. One of them cut off a branch and made a fine flute. But when he played the flute all that

came out was: "Czar Trojan has the ears of a goat! Czar Trojan has the
ears of a goat! Czar Trojan has the ears of a goat!"

The shepherds began to laugh. "Czar Trojan has the ears of goat!"
Immediately they set off for town to tell the news. "Czar Trojan has the
ears of a goat! Czar Trojan has the ears of a goat! Czar Trojan has the
ears of a goat!" they said to all who would listen.

The news spread like wildfire, and soon Czar Trojan himself heard
little children in the streets imitating the voice of the flute as it
whistled, "Czar Trojan has the ears of a goat!"

The czar was, to say the least, very angry. He immediately sent for
the apprentice because he was the only person in the world who knew
his secret. When the apprentice arrived, the czar demanded, "Why have
you told my secret to my people?"

"Sire, I swear I have not told a living soul," answered the frightened
apprentice. But he did confess that he had told his secret to the earth.
He told Czar Trojan how the elder tree had grown up on the spot
where he had confided the secret, and he recounted the story of how
each flute made from a branch of the tree whistled the secret to the
wind.

The czar, although you would not think it, was a kind-hearted man
and was very fond of his young barber, so he decided to test the truth
of the apprentice's words. Calling for his carriage and taking the
apprentice with him, he went in search of the elder tree.

When they arrived at the tree they discovered it only had one
branch left. Czar Trojan ordered the apprentice to make a flute, and
when it was made, he commanded the apprentice to play it. As the czar
listened in disbelief, the flute whistled, "Czar Trojan has the ears of a
goat! Czar Trojan has the ears of a goat! Czar Trojan has the ears of a
goat!"

That day Czar Trojan learned an important lesson: No secret can
remain hidden forever.[3]

Reflections on the Story

Fear causes even the most honorable people to hide. Fear caused the
women in Mark to remain silent and flee; fear caused the disciples to
deny they ever knew Jesus. This same fear still causes many a "good"
Christian today to remain silent rather than offend or upset someone else.
The story of "Czar Trojan's Ears" can be very helpful for young people
just coming to terms with fear. It can help not only those who are dealing

with the fear of telling someone about Jesus, but also those who are dealing with fears about such things as abuse.

The barber's apprentice is not the only person in this story who is afraid to tell what he or she knows. In most cases the young people will relate to Czar Trojan's fear. We all understand this fear. Everyone at one time or another has had something they have tried to hide from the world. It may be a speech impediment or poverty, but hiding from the world is a universal condition. Hiding the fact that one is a Christian is also a universal truism. Just as Peter denied Jesus in the courtyard, we have denied to others that we are in fact Christian. Although most Christians have done this, we can take heart in the message of the angel and the flute: Nothing on earth can remain hidden.

"Czar Trojan's Ears" is a great story and conveys the biblical message very well. However, there are times when the children need to hear *the* story, and Easter may be one of those times. But to just read the story from the Bible will not necessarily help the children to understand its meaning. Therefore, I have included an original retelling of the Mark empty tomb story that tells *the* story, yet offers meaning at a level the children can understand.

A RETELLING OF THE BIBLICAL TEXT ━━━━━━━━━━━━

Even the Trees Whisper His Name

Long ago there was a day that was longer than any other day. It was a day so long that it felt like three days. It all began at noon one Friday. There is one who still remembers that longest of days. And even today She stands as a silent witness to those events so very long ago, stretching out her leafy branches and shading the spot. But one day She told me her story.

"I was just a young oak tree then," She whispered into my ear. "It all began when the sky became as dark as night about lunch time. It was so dark that you needed a torch to see across the garden, and all the birds came home to their nests to sleep because they thought it was bedtime.

"For three hours it was pitch black, and the only sound that could be heard was the chirping of the crickets. Then out of the night a cry like I had never heard before, or since, broke the silence, and once again the sun shined, but not quite as brightly as before."

As She told me this, her limbs went a bit limp, heavy with sadness.

"It wasn't long after that, a man was carried into the garden of Joseph of Arimathea. Joseph himself helped three women carry the man's body and placed it in the grave. The four were in such a hurry, they didn't even have time to clean his body and say the proper prayers for him. You see, the real night was falling fast, bringing with it the Sabbath. On the Sabbath no one is allowed to work in any way. I heard the women saying something about coming back early Sunday morning to finish the burial. Then Joseph rolled a huge stone in front of the grave. The women and Joseph were crying and mourning loudly when they left."

She then began to shake and quiver almost as if she was crying, too.

"I heard them say the name of the one they buried. I heard them say the name of Jesus, Jesus," She repeated as the sound of the wind rustled through her leaves. Then She continued her story, "All night long I stood guard over the grave and the next day, too. It was a day that never seemed to end. The clouds hung low and the sky was grey, never letting the sun peek out, not even once. The town was not its usual hustle and bustle, and not a single family came to the garden for a picnic, which hundreds always did on the Sabbath. There was a sadness in the air. Even I felt it, but I didn't know why.

"Finally, the longest day ended. And the next morning the sunrise was the most beautiful I have ever seen. It was like something new had happened. Something glorious!"

As She said this her whole being seemed to bloom and blossom.

"Just as the three women said they would, they returned. They carried spices, clean linens, and oil so they could prepare the body of Jesus for a proper burial. I must have fallen asleep sometime during the night, because the huge stone was not in front of the grave. It had been rolled away! The women were just as surprised as I was.

"The three women tiptoed into the grave. Then I heard them shriek, 'AHHHH!' Then I saw him, too, a young man all dressed in white sitting beside where the body was supposed to be. It was an angel. I had never seen an angel before, but somehow I knew it was an angel. I knew because of the gentle way he talked and told the women not to be afraid.

"Then the angel said the strangest thing. He said, 'You are looking for Jesus of Nazareth, the one who was crucified and killed. He is not here. Jesus has been raised.' When he said this all of my sadness left, and I have never been so happy in all my life, but the three women still seemed scared. Then the angel told them, 'Go to Jesus' disciples and Peter and tell them that Jesus has gone ahead of them to their home town just like he told them he would.'

"After the angel told the women this they came running out of the grave as if they had seen a ghost. They were as white as sheets and scared speechless. I thought they would be happy, too."

The wind whistled through her branches as She paused.

"They were so afraid, I am not sure if they ever told anyone. I guess they were afraid something terrible might happen to them. Maybe the angel knew this, too, because before he left he blew upon me, and when his breath rustled my leaves, this message came forth, 'Jesus, Jesus, Jesus is risen!'

"You see," She continued, "some messages are too important to be kept secret. And that is why I tell this story to you, so you can tell others."

And this is why I tell you this story, so you, too, can tell others.

It is said that that old oak tree still stands on that spot, ready to tell her story. And if you listen closely when the wind blows through her leaves, you can still hear her softly whispering, "Jesus, Jesus, Jesus is risen."[4]

NOTES

[1] Pheme Perkins, "The Gospel of Mark," in *The New Interpreter's Bible*, vol. 8 (Nashville: Abingdon Press, 1995), p. 728; also see Lamar Williamson, Jr., *Mark* (Louisville: John Knox Press, 1983), p. 283; and Eduard Schweizer, *The Good News According to Mark*, translated by David E. Green (Atlanta: John Knox Press, 1974), p. 365f.

[2] Williamson, *Mark*, p. 286.

[3] A Slavic folktale.

[4] An original story by Donna L. Maison and Jeff Maison, 1997.

11

Tongue Meat

Psalm 30   **Week 3 of Easter, Year C**

I will extol you, O LORD, for you have drawn me up, and did not let my foes rejoice over me. O LORD my God, I cried to you for help, and you have healed me. O LORD, you brought up my soul from Sheol, restored me to life from among those gone down to the Pit.

Sing praises to the LORD, O you his faithful ones, and give thanks to his holy name. For his anger is but for a moment; his favor is for a lifetime. Weeping may linger for the night, but joy comes with the morning.

As for me, I said in my prosperity, "I shall never be moved." By your favor, O LORD, you had established me as a strong mountain; you hid your face; I was dismayed.

To you, O LORD, I cried, and to the LORD I made supplication: "What profit is there in my death, if I go down to the Pit? Will the dust praise you? Will it tell of your faithfulness? Hear, O LORD, and be gracious to me! O LORD, be my helper!"

You have turned my mourning into dancing; you have taken off my sackcloth and clothed me with joy, so that my soul may praise you and not be silent. O LORD my God, I will give thanks to you forever.

Comments on the Text

Every lectionary text has importance for children, a message that they need to hear. However, there are a few texts that are of special importance and significance to children and to their parents. Psalm 30 is one of those texts. The message of praise is of critical concern for the development of a child's emotional, physical, and spiritual life. We need to receive praise as well as give praise. For without praise in our lives, life becomes a living hell. The psalmist reminds us that life is about praise and being praised, and without praise there is no life.

Psalm 30 is one of the few psalms associated with a specific occasion. The superscript identifies it with the celebration of the dedication of the temple, or the Feast of Dedication commonly called Hanukkah.[1] There is some scholarly debate as to when this psalm of praise began to be associated with the temple dedication. Whether it was first used by the Maccabees to rededicate the temple in 165 B.C.E. after the desecration by Antiochus IV Epiphanes or used by the those who returned from the Babylonian captivity to rededicate the temple is not as important as it is to understand that Psalm 30 is a psalm of pure praise.

The praise offered to YHWH is one of thanksgiving, for bringing the psalmist out of great suffering and into renewed vitality. It is probably for this reason that the rabbinical school began to use it as thanksgiving for the restoration of the temple. Here most scholars agree, the psalm was most likely a prayer of celebration by a person who had recovered from an illness.[2] The psalm can be divided into five literary sections: Verse 1 is the statement of purpose; verses 2–5 are the basic thanksgiving for what has been done by God; verses 6–7 describe the crisis that the psalmist was in prior to God's deliverance; verses 8–10 is a quote from the prayer for help by the psalmist in distress; and verses 11–12 are the psalmist's confession of who has turned "mourning into dancing."

In the opening words, "I will extol you, O LORD" (30:1), we discover the intent and purpose of the prayer. The Hebrew verb used here, translated as "extol," literally means "to draw up" or "to lift up a bucket of water from the well."[3] It is used here to remind the reader that it is YHWH who has lifted the psalmist up out of the "Pit of Sheol" (30:3) and restored life. Thus, the psalm is a prayer of thanksgiving to YHWH, who has lifted up and given salvation to one who was on the brink of death. This idea is magnified in verses 2 and 3, where the psalmist acknowledges that life was on the brink of collapse, and it is YHWH and only YHWH who has "healed me" (30:2).

The psalmist recognizes the importance of the communal act of praise. All of YHWH's "faithful ones" are invited to "sing praises to YHWH" (30:4). The psalmist has discovered that the task of the living is praise and thanksgiving (30:3). In asking the community to join in singing praises and giving thanks, the psalmist becomes a witness to others about YHWH's character. The psalmist proclaims that YHWH is the God of "life" (30:3), and has committed to a lifetime of "favor" (30:5). That is, human suffering is not about "weeping" (30:5), but is ultimately about "joy."[4] The proof of this understanding is found in the psalmist's own realization of dependence on YHWH (30:6–7). The psalmist's "prosperity" did not include an understanding of life from YHWH (30:6); thus the psalmist cannot see YHWH and is struck down.

We are then told by the psalmist what was said to YHWH, who in turn "restored me to life" (30:3). Twice the psalmist pleads for mercy from YHWH (30:8, 10), and this forms the basis for the questions in verse 9. The questions should be heard as the psalmist's desire to live. Death is the loss of praise.[5] If one is to die, then one is not able to praise YHWH. The psalmist appears to be playing on YHWH's self-interest, or need for praise. It is as if the psalmist is attempting to bargain with YHWH: You need praise, but if I die I cannot offer you praise." However, the second plea to "be gracious" (30:10) mediates the idea of YHWH's selfishness. What at first appears to the readers to be a defect in the character of YHWH is transformed into a reminder of YHWH's graciousness. Thus, we are reminded that it is YHWH who is indeed the author of life.

This discovery of life transforms the life of the psalmist forever. No longer will suffering be a burden and a cause of mourning, but it will instead become a cause for "dancing" and "joy" (30:11). We should not make the mistake of thinking that praise will eliminate all suffering. Suffering is as much a part of life as praise. But because of being able to praise and be praised, suffering can become a source of rejoicing. The psalmist now understands that even in suffering YHWH is present, which makes suffering bearable. Therefore, the psalmist pledges to praise and give thanks "forever" (30:12). Not only will praise be a constant with the psalmist, but witnessing will also be constant. The psalmist will no longer "be silent" (30:12) but will become a vocal witness for YHWH.

Life and death are played against each other throughout this psalm. The question must be asked, "Why is death such a threatening place, and why does the psalmist fear it so much?" The answer is in its silence. For in death there is silence and in silence there can be no praise. One cannot live without praise. Salvation, then, is found in the ability to praise, for praise is truly life.

Tongue Meat

The sultan's wife was thin and very unhappy. No matter how many great riches the sultan gave her, nor how much of the finest foods her servants fed her, she remained lean and listless. This greatly upset the sultan, because he did not know how to please her.

Now it happened that near the sultan's palace lived a very poor man whose wife was plump and happy. So the sultan invited the poor man to visit him and asked him, "How is it that your wife is so plump, joyous, and healthy? Tell me, what is the secret of her happiness?"

The poor man replied, "It is no secret, your highness! Everyday I nourish my happy wife by feeding her *meat of the tongue.*"

"Aha!" cried the sultan, quite pleased to discover such a simple solution. He then immediately ordered his cook to buy and prepare the tongue of every animal he could find. And for days the sultan's wife was given tongue meat prepared in savory sauces. But no matter how much she ate, the sultan's wife remained thin and sad.

Finally the sultan came to the poor man and demanded that he exchange wives with him. Despite the poor man's objections, he had no choice but to obey the sultan, and the poor man's wife was taken to the palace and the sultan's own thin, sad wife was taken to the poor man's home.

No sooner had the poor man's wife arrived at the palace, but she too became sad and grew thinner and thinner with each passing day. In just a few short weeks the poor man's wife had lost her happiness, and her beauty faded like a wilted rose.

But at the poor man's home the sultan's wife grew happier and began to gain weight, despite the simple and meager meals. For you see, each night at sunset when the poor man would return from his work, he would tell his new wife all the funny and happy things that had happened to him during the day. He would make her laugh with joy, sing her songs of love, and share with her his deepest thoughts and concerns. And oftentimes they would end each night with dancing and stories.

During the day the poor man's new wife would laugh as she thought about the funny things her new husband had told her the night before. Within a few short weeks the poor man's new wife grew plump, her hair began to shine, and her skin glowed with new health.

One day the sultan saw his old wife and the poor man walking in the market and was amazed at the transformation that had occurred. "What has this poor man given you that I, a great and mighty sultan, cannot give? What has caused this sudden and dramatic change in you?" he asked his old wife.

The wife told the sultan how she and her new husband passed each evening together in story, song, and dance. Then the sultan's eyes filled with understanding, and he left the couple to their happiness, for he now knew what the poor man had meant when he said he fed his wife *meat of the tongue.*[6]

Reflections on the Story

Praise is life, and without praise a person shrivels up and dies. For years scientists and junior high science classes all over the world have proven the effects of praise on plants. A plant subjected to praise, kind words, and soft music thrives. A plant subjected to isloation and silence soon wilts. A plant subjected to harsh words and hateful feelings withers and dies quickly. The same is true for people. As the psalmist suffered and went down into the pit, so also the sultan and his wives suffer. It is not until the poor man helps transform the sultan's first wife into a happy and fulfilled person through praise, does the sultan realize that only in praise can there truly be life. We, too, must understand what the psalmist understood, and like the psalmist we must also determine to tell all that will hear; our children must be fed and taught to feed others and God "meat of the tongue" every day. For without praise we, too, will soon go down into the pit and become dust.

NOTES

[1] J. Clinton McCann, Jr., "The Book of Psalms," *The New Interpreter's Bible,* vol. 4 (Nashville: Abingdon Press, 1996), p. 795; also see James Luther Mays, *Psalms* (Louisville: John Knox Press, 1994), p. 140.

[2] McCann, "The Book of Psalms," p. 795, and Mitchell Dahood, *Psalm I: 1–50* (The Anchor Bible; Garden City, N.Y.: Doubleday, 1966), p. 182.

[3] McCann, "The Book of Psalms," p. 796, and Dahood, *Psalms I*, p. 182.

[4] McCann, "The Book of Psalms," p. 796.

[5] Mays, *Psalms*, p. 141.

[6] A Swahili east-central African folktale.

12

Salt and Bread

Acts 11:1–18   **Week 5 of Easter, Year C**

*Now the apostles and the believers who were in Judea heard that the Gentiles had
also accepted the word of God. So when Peter went up to Jerusalem, the circumcised believers criticized him, saying, "Why did you go to uncircumcised men and
eat with them?" Then Peter began to explain it to them, step by step, saying, "I was
in the city of Joppa praying, and in a trance I saw a vision. There was something
like a large sheet coming down from heaven, being lowered by its four corners; and
it came close to me. As I looked at it closely I saw four-footed animals, beasts of
prey, reptiles, and birds of the air. I also heard a voice saying to me, 'Get up, Peter;
kill and eat.' But I replied, 'By no means, Lord; for nothing profane or unclean has
ever entered my mouth.' But a second time the voice answered from heaven, 'What
God has made clean, you must not call profane.' This happened three times; then
everything was pulled up again to heaven. At that very moment three men, sent to
me from Caesarea, arrived at the house where we were. The Spirit told me to go
with them and not to make a distinction between them and us. These six brothers
also accompanied me, and we entered the man's house. He told us how he had seen
the angel standing in his house and saying, 'Send to Joppa and bring Simon, who
is called Peter; he will give you a message by which you and your entire household
will be saved.' And as I began to speak, the Holy Spirit fell upon them just as it
had upon us at the beginning. And I remembered the word of the Lord, how he had*

said, 'John baptized with water, but you will be baptized with the Holy Spirit.' If then God gave them the same gift that he gave us when we believed in the Lord Jesus Christ, who was I that I could hinder God?" When they heard this, they were silenced. And they praised God, saying, "Then God has given even to the Gentiles the repentance that leads to life."

Comments on the Text

With the exception of a few extreme people, most consider themselves to be loving and accepting of anyone who is different. "I haven't a prejudiced bone in my body," is the phrase most often repeated. Christians in particular tend to have a high moral conception of themselves as non-prejudiced people. After all, we are followers of Jesus, the one who associated with the lowest of the low. Yet, the reality is that more often than not we do not realize the extent of our own prejudices. It is not until we are placed in intimate circumstances that we discover that we, too, are prejudiced. Sharing meals with others tells us more about our prejudice than any other set of circumstances. It is a question of who we are willing to eat with, and who are we are not willing to eat with. It is this division between who can come to the Lord's table and who cannot that is the major stumbling block to Christian unity. Even the apostles and the early Christians had to learn to overcome their prejudices in order to truly share in the Lord's supper.

The scripture text is the final scene of a much larger story (Acts 10:1—11:18), chronicling the church's development toward a more inclusive fellowship. Before we move farther into the story itself, the point needs to be made that what we are talking about is not just any meal. Today we separate Sunday dinner from worship; the two have no commonality. However, this was not the case for Christians in the first centuries, where worship and a full meal were one and the same.[1] At issue then is who can or cannot participate in the Lord's supper. Much like ourselves today, the early church's prejudice does not come to the surface until they have to eat together. Baptizing and spreading the good news of Jesus Christ to the Gentiles was not objectionable. Problems arose when these new converts were brought into the fellowship, which meant Jews and Gentiles alike would have to eat together, in direct opposition to what they had been taught was right and proper all their lives.[2]

Many consider this story the turning point for the early church, because it is the point at which the gospel truly began to be preached to "all nations" (Matt. 28:19). There is a strange dualism that runs throughout this story. The reader is constantly reminded of previous stories told in the writer's first work, Luke. The story begins with the introduction of a

Gentile centurion named Cornelius, who sends messengers to ask for an audience with Peter (Acts 10:1). Immediately the reader is reminded of another devout centurion in need, who also sent messengers to ask for an audience with Jesus (Luke 7:2–10).

While the messengers travel, Peter goes to the roof of the house where he is staying to pray. In prayer Peter falls into a "trance" and receives a vision from the Holy Spirit. In this vision Peter sees "all kinds of four-footed animals, beasts of prey, reptiles, and birds of the air" (10:12). A voice, later identified as the Holy Spirit, instructs Peter to "get up...kill and eat" (10:13). But Peter refuses to obey, citing his obedience to the purity and dietary laws of Judaism. Peter refuses to obey the command not once, not twice, but three times (10:16). Again the reader is reminded of earlier stories. First, of Peter's previous refusal to acknowledge Jesus during the trial (Luke 22:54–62). The reader may also be reminded of Jesus' three refusals of Satan during the wilderness temptations (Luke 4:1–13). Whether the author intended there to be a connection between the two or not is unclear. Clearly, though, we are intended to understand that Peter took his religious practices seriously and that to overcome those cultural norms was no easy task, even for the Holy Spirit.

Peter then goes to Caesarea with the messengers and some other believers from Joppa. Greeting Cornelius, Peter explains why he was able to come to the house of a Gentile despite the prohibition against it (10:28–29). The imminent movement to a truly Gentile mission comes in verse 34. It is also a verse that we as Christians should hold dear today, "I truly understand that God shows no partiality." With this the Holy Spirit falls upon the gathered Gentiles in the same manner as described at the Pentecost event (Acts 2:1–13). The "circumcised believers" are astounded by this manifestation of the spirit. Peter uses this event as proof that all, Jew and Gentile alike, are able to receive the gospel, and thus he baptizes the household of Cornelius and stays and has fellowship with them for "several days" (Acts 10:48).

It is this strange turn of events that sets the stage for the text at hand. Peter returns to Jerusalem, where word of his actions has proceeded him (Acts 11:1). The Jewish believers have questions for Peter, and Peter must now answer for what he has done. The issue for the Jerusalem church, however, is not about preaching the gospel, nor about baptizing Gentiles, but is about eating with "uncircumcised men" (Acts 11:3). Peter's defense is a detailed retelling of the events in chapter 10.

Who then is welcome at the Lord's table? Peter answers this question rather succinctly for all of us, "If God gave them the same gift that he gave us when we believed in the Lord Jesus Christ, who was I that I could hinder God?" (Acts 11:17). In stunned silence the church contemplates what has happened. A new and frightening journey has begun for the young church, for now they realize that God has granted to Gentiles and Jews alike the ability to turn toward life, "and they praised God" (Acts 11:18).

Who then is welcome at the Lord's table? The story puts an effective end to all prejudices, especially during table fellowship. If there is a litmus test for inclusion at the Lord's table, it would appear to be belief in the Lord Jesus Christ (Acts 11:17). But then again, who are we to hinder God?

CHILDREN'S SERMON ───────────────────────────

Salt and Bread

There once lived a king who had three daughters. The older daughters were jealous of the youngest, because the king loved her very much. They were always telling the king that their younger sister did not love him and she was not worthy of his love. Their evil jealousy and mean rumors began to trouble the king, and he started to become suspicious of his youngest daughter.

So one day when all four were together, the king decided to conduct a little test. He asked his oldest daughter to describe to him how much she loved him, and she answered:

"Oh father, I love you as much as I love our God."

This pleased the king very much. He then asked the same question of his second daughter, who answered:

"Oh father, I love you as much as I love my own life."

This also pleased the king very much. Now he turned to his youngest daughter and asked the same question, and she answered:

"Oh father, I love you as much as I love salt and bread."

This angered the king very much! "How dare she compare her love for me with mere salt and bread!" he raged. The king believed that the young girl cared no more for him than she did for the most common items, items that even the poorest of homes had on their dinner tables every night. The king became furious with his youngest daughter and ordered her out of the palace that very night.

The king ordered his servants to take her out to the forest and leave her there to fend for herself. The servants did as they were ordered. And what of the two sisters? Why, they were quite pleased with themselves and what they had accomplished.

Left all by herself in the forest, the youngest daughter became frightened. She could not understand why her father, whom she loved so much, was so angry with her. And she could find no reason at all as to why she was being banished from her home.

For days the young daughter wandered around the forest, broken-hearted. She could not sleep for worry and fear and had found nothing to eat. Sleep and hunger began to overtake her, and soon the young daughter began to imagine that wild animals would eat her. And so she climbed into a tall tree to protect herself.

At about that same time there was a king from another country hunting in the forest where the young daughter had been left to die. The young king, following his barking dogs, was led to the tree in which the princess had climbed. The dogs barked and yapped so much that the king was sure he would find a beautiful ermine hiding in the tree. But when he looked up into the tree what he saw was the very beautiful face of the very unhappy princess.

The young king was a kind man, and he asked her to come out of the tree. When she did, he put her on his horse and took her to his castle. There he fed her and took care of her. Overcome by his kindness and her own sadness, she finally told him the whole story of how she came to be in the forest.

The young king took care of her for a long time, and eventually the two fell in love and agreed to be married.

A date was set for the wedding, and invitations were sent to all the neighboring kingdoms. All the royal guests arrived on the wedding day. Among the royal guests were the young princess' father and two older sisters, but they did not recognize her, for they thought she had died long ago in the forest.

To celebrate the wedding a great feast was prepared. Exotic birds and animals from near and far were prepared, and soups and salads of every kind were served. But none of the food was salted, and there was no salt on the table, and neither was there any bread. Finally, the young daughter's father could not keep from commenting and said, "I don't understand, but it seems to me that the two most precious items are missing from this feast."

The princess, now a queen, answered, "What do you mean, sire?"

"Why, there is no salt, nor is there bread," her father told her.

"I agree with you, sire; I, too, believe that salt and bread are among the most precious things we know. And once long ago I told my father I loved him as I do salt and bread. But because I only loved him as much as these two precious items, he banished me from his house and left me in the forest to die alone."

When the old king heard these words, he was overcome with happiness and sadness at the same time. He hugged her with joy, thankful that she was alive and well and asked her to forgive him for the wrong he had done to her.

And what of the two wicked, older sisters? Their plot was discovered, and this time it was they who were banished from their home and left in the forest. But they were never rescued by kings hunting in the forest and were never heard from again.[3]

Reflections on the Story

Prejudice seems to manifest itself most deeply at the dinner table. Who we will eat with and who we will not are important issues for most people. Some believe the importance is found in our vulnerability at the table, while others contend that it signifies equality of status to dine together. Whatever the case may be, prejudice eats at the individual and society and stunts the growth of both the host and the potential guest. After Peter's revelation and explanation of events at Cornelius' home, the Jewish Christian community understood that for the gospel to grow they had to discard their prejudices and truly love all others, just as Jesus had taught them.

The story is a perfect allegory for what is happening among the Jewish Christians in this text. In their jealousy the two older daughters plot against the younger, determined to keep their father's love all for themselves. The Jerusalem Christians appeared to be doing much the same in the Acts story, using table fellowship as a means to keep the Gentiles at arm's length from God. The young daughter understood that love can best be expressed in table fellowship and uses the metaphor of salt and bread to demonstrate that understanding. Yet, her father does not understand this expression of love and banishes her from the table to fend for herself in the dark forest. The Gentiles were not totally excluded, for they could certainly be baptised. However, they were banished from Christ's table to fend for themselves, left to grope in the dark. That is, until a dashing young king comes along to rescue them.

Peter is sent out by the Holy Spirit to "hunt" for new converts. In Peter's search he comes to realize that his prejudices make no difference to God. They are his problems, not God's. For God is able to choose any and all, and does. The young daughter had every reason in the world to forbid her family access to the table but chose not to. Instead, in a visual, and textual way she demonstrates to her father the importance of her words spoken so long ago. With this realization the old king repents of his poor judgment and is forgiven by his young daughter. Opening the Lord's table will be impossible for us, until we are able to open our own tables in love to all of God's children.

NOTES

[1] Richard Pervo, *Acts* (Nashville: Abingdon, 1997), p. 40; also see William H. Willimon, *Acts* (Louisville: John Knox Press, 1988), p. 99.

[2] Pervo, *Acts*, p. 40.

[3] A Swedish folktale.

13

The Most Beautiful Thing in the World

Acts 2:1–13   **Pentecost Sunday, Year A**

When the day of Pentecost had come, they were all together in one place. And suddenly from heaven there came a sound like the rush of a violent wind, and it filled the entire house where they were sitting. Divided tongues, as of fire, appeared among them, and a tongue rested on each of them. All of them were filled with the Holy Spirit and began to speak in other languages, as the Spirit gave them ability. Now there were devout Jews from every nation under heaven living in Jerusalem. And at this sound the crowd gathered and was bewildered, because each one heard them speaking in the native language of each. Amazed and astonished, they asked, "Are not all these who are speaking Galileans? And how is it that we hear, each of us, in our own native language? Parthians, Medes, Elamites, and residents of Mesopotamia, Judea and Cappadocia, Pontus and Asia, Phrygia and Pamphylia, Egypt and the parts of Libya belonging to Cyrene, and visitors from Rome, both Jews and proselytes, Cretans and Arabs—in our own languages we hear them speaking about God's deeds of power." All were amazed and perplexed, saying to one another, "What does this mean?" But others sneered and said, "They are filled with new wine."

Comments on the Text

Pentecost is celebrated as the birthday or the beginning of the church of Jesus Christ, and the Acts of the Apostles' story is traditionally the story Christians use to focus on the celebration. Why should this event be the focus? Why not the great commission (Matthew 28:18–20)? or the ascension story (Acts 1:3–11) that is told just before the Pentecost account? I do not argue with the tradition, but there is more we can learn from the Pentecost story than just the founding of the church.

All the disciples—whether this means the twelve (including the newly elected Matthias, 1:26) or the 120 is unclear—have gathered together in a house to celebrate the Feast of Weeks. This Jewish festival acquired the Greek name Pentecost, because it was observed fifty days after Passover. While they celebrated this Jewish festival, a dramatic event occurred. "Suddenly" a "sound like the rush of a violent wind" (2:2) came through the room and created a great stir among those present. The Greek word is translated as "wind" here, but it is also the same Greek word that is translated "spirit" throughout the New Testament. It is possible the author of Acts intended the reader to interpret the wind that is heard as the same creating "wind" of Genesis 1, informing the reader that God is again creating something new.[1]

The wind that is first heard is then seen in the form of "divided tongues, as of fire" (2:3). Verse 4 is the explanation that the wind and the fire are none other than the promised Spirit (1:8), fulfilling the prophecy of John the Baptizer who said that "He will baptize you with the Holy Spirit and fire" (Luke 3:16). The Spirit gives to those assembled in the room the gift of "tongues" (2:4). It is at this point that scholars become divided concerning the interpretation of the Pentecost event. Is the glossolalia (speaking in tongues) described here in Acts 2:4 to be understood as the same ecstatic speech described by Paul in 1 Corinthians 12 and 14 and also described in Acts 10:46 and 19:6?[2] The content of the text makes this interpretation doubtful. Paul, in 1 Corinthians, makes it clear that glossolalia of the ecstatic kind must have an interpreter; otherwise the glossolalia is unintelligible to humans (1 Corinthians 14:27–28). Ecstatic glossolalia is described by Paul as the language of "angels" and is not human speech (1 Corinthians 13:1). In the Acts 2 account we are told that the hearers of this glossolalia are able to understand the speech without the assistance of an interpreter. The people who gathered in the room could not only "speak in other languages," but people from all over the world who were in Jerusalem celebrating the festival were "amazed and astonished" that they could hear their "own native language" (2:7). As

William Willimon explains, the "concern is with the description of a Spirit-empowered intelligible proclamation in foreign languages (2:6, 8)."[3]

Acts records a language miracle, but what is the reason behind reporting a miracle of spontaneous world-wide communication? Some scholars believe this is the reversal of Babel (Genesis 11:1–9). The single language of the world that was confused and divided into a multitude of languages at Babel is now reversed, and the whole world once again understands. However, a single language is not used by the people gathered in the room, but a multitude of languages are used (2:9–11). Others see it as an event similar to that described in the rabbinic tradition of the language miracle at Sinai "in which the voice of God divided itself into seventy world languages and the law was made known to all nations, but only Israel accepted it."[4] The connection between the beginning of Israel and the beginning of the church is clearly evident, although the evidence of such a connection has to be found outside of the Pentecost story itself.

To clearly understand the importance of this event we need to move farther into the story. From the inbreaking of the Spirit that occurs in private, the scene moves outside the room and into the street, where a crowd has gathered. Whether the crowd gathers because of the commotion made by the Spirit or because of the multitude of languages heard coming from the room is unclear. The crowd is made up of "devout Jews from every nation under heaven" (2:5). The crowd is both "bewildered" and "amazed and astonished" at what they hear coming from the Galileans. The crowd's reactions are easier to comprehend, and our appreciation of the miracle is deepened, when we realize the difficulty other Jews from Palestine had in understanding the normal Galilean accent. The Galilean accent was heavy with the indistinct pronunciation of guttural consonants. It was "a dialect in which syllables were often swallowed in such a way that the meaning of words and phrases often became doubtful to a southern Jew."[5] The confusion then is that they are able to understand a group of Galileans clearly speaking in their native language.

The Spirit empowers the disciples to speak in "all" the known languages of the world. This is evident by the laundry list of nations provided by the author. There has been much discussion as to the source of this list. Is it an astrological catalogue similar to that of Paulus Alexandrinus, or some other established list of nations? It is more likely that the author wants to include as many nations as possible in which Jews lived to give support to the idea that "Jews from every nation under heaven" were present in the crowd. Another function of the list of nations that accompanies the story is to demonstrate the global and universal nature of the gospel that is and will be proclaimed. However, it should be noted that the Gentile mission of the church is not apparent in this story because the crowd is not filled with people of all nations but is filled with Jews of all nations. The whole world can again hear the good news of God. But unlike what happened at Sinai, where God's own voice proclaimed the good news, at Pentecost God is sending people out into the world to proclaim God's good news.

The varied reactions of the crowd set up a recurring theme in Acts. While some in the crowd are "amazed," others sneer and mock the disciples, saying, "They are filled with new wine" (2:13), or in other words, drunk. Some will accept what has happened without question; others are intrigued to seek more; while others reject the miracle out of hand, finding some logical rationale (they must be drunk) to account for what is happening. In the same way as in Luke, the author uses miracles as a means for proclamation. For the author, it is not the miracle itself that is important but the ability and opportunity to proclaim the good news that is of utmost importance. Because the miracle occurred, an opportunity to proclaim the good news of Jesus Christ is available to Jesus' disciples.

The language miracle not only empowered the disciples in the room to move out into the world to proclaim the gospel but also empowers all Christians to move out into the world. The scene is set for the movement of the good news from the confines of Judea and Jerusalem to the rest of the world, to the very gates of Rome (2:10). The language miracle of Pentecost is retold by the writer of Luke and Acts to empower Christians, then and now, to proclaim the good news with confidence. Christians can proclaim the good news with the certainty that some people will be "amazed" and understand what they hear, some will be "perplexed," and still others will sneer. William Willimon states: "The Spirit is the power which enables the church to 'go public' with its good news, to attract a crowd and...to have something to say worth hearing."[6]

CHILDREN'S SERMON ————————————————————

The Most Beautiful Thing in the World

One day, the king of Yong-An called his three sons to him. "My sons, I am growing old," he said. "Soon I must choose one of you to wear my crown. So I have decided to hold a contest. The one who brings me the most beautiful thing in the world will win the crown."

The king gave each son one hundred gold coins and told them, "You have nine days. Go. Seek. Find."

The princes bowed, then hurried away.

On a white horse, the oldest prince chose to seek the most beautiful thing in the world in the markets of the cities. He rode from one market town to another, seeking but not finding. He fingered tasseled tapestries, stroked silken robes, but saw nothing worthy of his father's throne.

Finally, on the ninth morning, he watched a painter finish the loveliest picture he had ever seen in his life. "Surely this must be the most beautiful thing in the world!" he said. And he quickly traded his gold for the painting and rode toward the palace.

On a black horse the middle prince chose to seek the most beautiful thing in the world in the country and mountains. He rode into the mountains, seeking but not finding. The last night, he saw white smoke and a light coming from a cave. Quiet as a shadow, he led his horse toward the light.

In the cave, he found an enormous dragon. Under the dragon's chin glowed a perfect pearl the size of a duck egg. "Surely this pearl is the most beautiful thing in the world!" the prince said. "But how shall I gain it?"

The prince knew that dragons never sell their treasures but would sometimes trade them for kindness. So that night, he caught and roasted nine swallows. At sunrise on the ninth day, the prince laid the swallows outside the cave as a gift for the dragon.

Hungrily, the dragon ate the swallows. After the dragon had eaten his fill he dropped the pearl at the prince's feet. Bowing to the dragon, the prince tucked the gleaming pearl into his sash. Then how he rode toward the palace!

Meanwhile, the youngest prince chose to seek the most beautiful thing in the world in heart of the capital city. He walked among his father's people, seeking beauty but finding only sadness and great need. He found people who only had ragged clothing to wear, and many cried from hunger, and some had no home but lived in the streets.

Wanting to help, the youngest son gave one gold coin after another to the people who were in need so that hungry people ate, those who wore ragged clothes bought new robes, and people who had no roof over their heads built homes. And very soon there was great joy in the city.

As the youngest prince gave away his last coin, his brothers came riding by. "Ah, foolish one, come with us," they said.

At the palace, the oldest son showed the painting to his father. "Magnificent!" said the king.

The middle prince showed the pearl to his father. "Perfect!" said the king.

The youngest prince hung his head in sadness and said, "Father, I am sorry, but I have no beautiful thing to show you."

"Ah, you are wrong, my son," said the king. "Word of your kindness has come to me daily." He smiled at his youngest son.

"You have shown me the most beautiful thing in the world—a caring heart. You deserve the crown," the king said.

Thus, the youngest prince became king and ruled long and with justice in Yong-An.[7]

Reflections on the Story

Before anyone is able to do anything, she or he must be empowered to attempt it. A child does not walk without first being encouraged to try and praised for every halting attempt. Even in the political arena politicians "test the waters" before running for an office or proposing legislation. We have a need to be empowered and encouraged to try new things, to know that there is some chance for success. God sent the Spirit on that first Pentecost to empower the followers of Jesus, then and today, to go forth into the world, or as William Willimon says, the Spirit is "the engine that drives the church into all the world."[8]

A story for this passage needs to have an element of going out into the world witnessing and proclaiming the deeds of Jesus. Witnessing and proclaiming, however, are not just verbal skills but are also action skills. We must remember that the children who sit with us on Sunday morning are at a developmental stage where seeing what is to be done is understood, whereas hearing about what is to be done is incomprehensible. "The Most Beautiful Thing in the World" offers a story of a young prince who is empowered to go out into the kingdom and be with the people. While he is with the people he not only sees their needs, but because he has been empowered, he does something about it. The prince's action *is* the Christian message that we have been taught: to "love the Lord your God with all your heart, and with all your soul, and with all your strength, and with all your mind; and your neighbor as yourself" (Luke 10:27)—which, of course, is the most beautiful thing in the world.

NOTES

[1] William H. Willimon, *Acts* (Louisville: John Knox Press, 1988), p. 30.

[2] Baird and Bruce contend the glossolalia in 2:4 is the same ecstatic speech as 1 Corinthians; see William Baird, "The Acts of the Apostles," in *Acts & Paul's Letters* (Nashville: Abingdon Press, 1983), p. 8; and F. F. Bruce, *The Acts of the Apostles: The Greek Text with Introduction and Commentary* (Chicago and Toronto: The InterVarsity Christian Fellowship, 1952), p. 82.

[3] Willimon, *Acts*, p. 32.

[4] Gerd Lüdemann, *Early Christianity According to the Traditions in Acts: A Commentary* (Minneapolis: Fortress Press, 1987), p. 39.

[5] Bruce, *The Acts of the Apostles*, p. 84.

[6] Willimon, *Acts*, p. 33.

[7] A Chinese folktale.

[8] Willimon, *Acts*, p. 32.

14

The Blue Jackal

I Kings 17:8–24   **Week 3 of Pentecost, Year C**

Then the word of the LORD came to him, saying, "Go now to Zarephath, which belongs to Sidon, and live there; for I have commanded a widow there to feed you." So he set out and went to Zarephath. When he came to the gate of the town, a widow was there gathering sticks; he called to her and said, "Bring me a little water in a vessel, so that I may drink." As she was going to bring it, he called to her and said, "Bring me a morsel of bread in your hand." But she said, "As the LORD your God lives, I have nothing baked, only a handful of meal in a jar, and little oil in a jug; I am now gathering a couple of sticks, so that I may go home and prepare it for myself and my son, that we may eat it, and die." Elijah said to her, "Do not be afraid; go and do as you have said; but first make me a little cake of it and bring it to me, and afterwards make something for yourself and your son. For thus says the LORD the God of Israel: The jar of meal will not be emptied and the jug of oil will not fail until the day that the LORD sends rain on the earth." She went and did as Elijah said, so that she as well as he and her household ate for many days. The jar of meal was not emptied, neither did the jug of oil fail, according to the word of the LORD that he spoke by Elijah.

After this the son of the woman, the mistress of the house, became ill; his illness was so severe that there was no breath left in him. She then said to Elijah, "What have you against me, O man of God? You have come to me to bring my sin to remembrance, and to cause the death of my son!" But he said to her, "Give me your son." He took him from her bosom, carried him up into the upper chamber where he was lodging, and laid him on his own bed. He cried out to the LORD, "O LORD my God, have you brought calamity even upon the widow with whom I am staying, by killing her son?" Then he stretched himself upon the child three times, and cried out to the LORD, "O LORD my God, let this child's life come into him again." The LORD listened to the voice of Elijah; the life of the child came into him again, and he revived. Elijah took the child, brought him down from the upper chamber into the house, and gave him to his mother; then Elijah said, "See, your son is alive." So the woman said to Elijah, "Now I know that you are a man of God, and that the word of the LORD in your mouth is truth."

Comments on the Text

I can remember as a child actively participating in the male ritual of one-upsmanship. In this male ritual, I and other young male children would prove our machismo by proudly declaring, "My dad is better than yours," or "My dad can whip your dad." In retrospect, this childish game proved nothing. No dad ever came out and fought another; it was merely a game of words, bragging about the power and love we had for our fathers. In 1 Kings the childish game of "my dad is better than yours" takes on supernatural proportions. Who is really the God of life; Baal or YHWH?

The two stories we have in this lectionary text are part of the larger overall story (1 Kings 17—19) of the confrontation between the Israelites who believed that the Yahweh religion was compatible with the Canaanite religion of Baal and those who believed the two religions were incompatible. In order for these two stories to make sense, it is necessary to step back and recall the events of the first 16 verses of the chapter. Elijah bursts on the scene out of nowhere; all that we are told is that he is from Gilead (17:1). The narrator does not provide us with any information as to Elijah's prophetical credentials. Instead the narrator lets the stories prove that Elijah is indeed a "man of God" (17:18, 24). Elijah is proven throughout the stories to be a true prophet of YHWH by his words, deeds, and actions, unlike the "false prophets" Elijah later unmasks (18:20–40).

This unknown man from the farthest reaches of Israel bursts in on King Ahab and demands that Israel repent of its breaking of the first commandment and acknowledge that YHWH alone is God. Ahab's refusal causes YHWH to impose a drought upon the land so that "there shall be neither dew nor rain these years, except by my word" (17:1). Choosing a drought is not an arbitrary punishment; it is a direct challenge to the god the Israelites have placed before YHWH. Baal was the Canaanite god of vegetation and rain. If Baal is God, then the rituals and prayers to

Baal will cause the rains to fall and end the drought. If, on the other hand, the drought continues and is only ended by the word of YHWH, then it is clear that YHWH is indeed God. It is implied that the drought angered Ahab and forced Elijah into hiding. Elijah would need to remain safe, for it is through him that the word of God will be spoken and so end the drought. Thus "the word of the Lord came to" (17:2) Elijah, commanding him to go into the wilderness. Throughout these three stories it is the word of God that is the main emphasis and focal point. It is only by the word of God that things happen.

It is Elijah's obedience to YHWH that leads him to the widow at Zarephath. YHWH directs Elijah to go "to Zarephath, which belongs to Sidon" (17:9), to the very heart of the Baal religion. The reader of this story is immediately reminded that Baal's champion, Jezebel, is also from Sidon. But even in the heart of Baal's realm, the vegetation god cannot feed the hungry nor provide water for the thirsty. The drought/famine is becoming acute, and death is imminent for those living in the kingdom. Elijah approaches the widow whom God has directed him to and politely asks for a drink of water, which the woman graciously proceeds to get for him. But just as the woman begins to leave, Elijah, asks for "a morsel of bread in your hand" (17:11). What some people may construe as an attempt by the widow to avoid giving Elijah food and drink is in reality the storyteller's way of explaining the extreme conditions of the widow when she simply states what her condition is. She has just enough meal, oil, and water for one last meal, then it will all be gone and they will then "die" (17:12). This should come as no surprise to anyone. The woman is a widow, and, unlike our society, there was no Aid to Dependent Families to help her in this time of crisis. This woman was all alone without anyone to provide for her and her son. What Elijah asked of her seemed an invitation to certain death through starvation.

Elijah's words of assurance to "not be afraid" (17:13) for YHWH will provide for all our needs, provides the basis for the widow's acceptance of YHWH's word and later for her conversion (17:24). The miracle that the meal and oil do not fail is a reminder that even in the midst of adversity, the word of God is able to supply one's needs. As Gene Rice notes, "Here in Baal's backyard, in the home of the weakest member of society, a demonstration of the power of the word of God is given."[1]

As time passes, yet another calamity befalls the widow woman. Saved from starvation, her son now falls ill. What the illness is, we do not know; what is certain is that the illness is mortal. We are never told that the boy actually dies but only that he is near death. This biological reality is of more importance to contemporary people, for the people who originally heard the story did not have the sharp distinction between life and death that we do now.[2] The point is that the boy was as good as dead. The widow naturally assumes the logical and cultural reason for death in one so young; punishment by a deity for past sins. She then blames Elijah for coming into her house and making YHWH aware of her existence, thus causing YHWH to know her sins and inflict punishment upon her son.

Elijah takes the boy and goes up to his own private room and immediately asks YHWH if it is in fact YHWH who has "brought calamity even upon the widow with whom I am staying?" (15:20). The focus of the story is not on some magical transfer of life-giving energy from Elijah to the boy through bodily contact. The text is clear here: YHWH responds not to Elijah's stretching out on the boy but "listened to the voice of Elijah" (17:22). The miracle is a matter of prayer and words. YHWH is proven once again to be the God of life, and the widow makes that confession of faith.

The battle between the Yahwehists and Baalists revolves around who is the God of life. The three stories of chapter 17 demonstrate that YHWH is the God of life and sets the stage for the climactic events at Mt. Carmel in chapter 18. In the first story YHWH controls life-giving rain. In the second story YHWH controls life by providing food and water. Finally, in the third story YHWH is shown to have absolute control over life and death. God is the God of life, not only of yesterday and tomorrow; the good news is that God is also the God of life, today.

CHILDREN'S SERMON ———————————————

The Blue Jackal

One day a scrawny jackal was very hungry. So he decided to leave his pack and crawl to a village in search of food. When he arrived at the village, a group of dogs found him and began to chase him through the village. The jackal dashed into the house of a cloth dyer. He ran hither and yon, turning over tables and pots and crashing dishes to the floor, and tumbled into a large vat of blue dye. The odor of the dye was so strong that the dogs did not find him in the vat, and so he stayed hidden there until the dogs finally left. Checking not once but twice, to be sure the dogs had truly left, the jackal crept back into the bush.

As he walked through the bush, animals all along the way gasped in admiration at his extraordinary color. The dye had changed his fur to a deep blue-purple. "What is this exotic animal; did he fall from the sky?"

they asked. Others said things like "He is the most beautiful animal in the world!" But all of them cowered in fear and awe of the Blue Jackal.

The Blue Jackal looked at himself and admired his beauty. Then a new thought came to his mind. In his most majestic voice he announced, "Creatures of the bush, gather around and hear my words! I am your new king!"

The astonishing news quickly spread throughout the bush as one animal informed the next, "A mysterious animal of royal color has fallen from the sky and is now our rightful ruler!" Very soon the news reached the real king. "Who is it that would take my place among the animals?" thought the Lion King. So he, too, joined all the other animals who gathered to pay homage to the new king.

The Blue Jackal was delighted that lions, cheetahs, leopards, monkeys, rabbits, jackals, gazelles, and others, big and small, now bowed before him. "Tell us our duties, O great king!" they pleaded.

The Blue Jackal began to give out jobs. In his best imitation of the Lion King he squeaked out his orders. He made the cheetahs his ministers, the leopards his guards; the monkeys took turns as the royal jesters, and the rabbits served his food. Every animal was given a royal task. Every animal, that is, except the jackals, who reminded him of his lowly origins.

Now, the Lion King watched as all this took place. Some might have wondered why the king did not just kill the pretender, for no jackal is a match for a lion. But the Lion King knew that if he did that, his royal subjects would no longer respect him. Instead, the king decided to wait and watch because he knew when real danger came to the bush, the jackal would show his true colors and run and hide like the coward he was.

So time passed and the Blue Jackal enjoyed the privileges of being king. When he was rude, crude, or socially unacceptable, no one challenged him. After all, he was their leader, and all the animals bore his ill manners with great tolerance and patience.

One day a mad elephant crashed through the bush. The elephant had been wounded, and the pain had driven him mad. He stampeded through the bush, destroying and killing everything in his path. As the Blue Jackal was berating and bullying the monkeys, the other animals came to the Blue Jackal. "O great king, do something, drive the mad elephant from us. Save us, great king!"

In the distance the Jackal saw the rogue elephant rushing toward him. But instead of being a courageous king, the Blue Jackal showed his true colors and ran screaming and hid behind a tree with his tail between his legs.

With a terrible crash, the elephant entered the royal grounds, terrifying the animals. And just as the elephant was about to reach out and grab a leopard with his mighty trunk, the Lion King leaped on the elephant with a mighty roar. And very soon after that the rogue elephant departed from the bush, never to return.

Now all the animals suddenly realized that their king of royal color was nothing but an ordinary jackal pretending to be what he was not. Outraged at the Blue Jackal's deception, the animals attacked him and drove him away. He tried to return to the other jackals, but they remembered how he had refused to welcome them when he was king, and now they refused to welcome him.

Alone and miserable, without a family or a community, the Blue Jackal crept into the shadows of his cave to lick his wounds.[3]

Reflections on the Story

It is human nature to seek out strong leadership. Even young children seek out and latch onto those who demonstrate love, care, and compassion. We just want to be taken care of. The Israelites of Elijah's time were no different from the animals in "The Blue Jackal." Both sought someone to care for them. In like manner, we are also fickle followers. We often choose to discard the old, reliable, dependable, and proven caretaker for what promises to be a new, more exciting provider. In our search for the new and improved we forget that life comes from one source and one source only—God. But God, like the Lion King, does not beat us into submission but waits patiently in the wings until we ask for "life to come again" (17:21).

NOTES

[1] Gene Rice, *Nations Under God: A Commentary on the Book of 1 Kings* (Grand Rapids: William B. Eerdmans Publishing, 1990), p. 143.

[2] Richard D. Nelson, *First and Second Kings* (Louisville: John Knox Press, 1987), p. 111.

[3] A North African folktale.

15

Could This Be Paradise?

Romans 6:1–11   **Week 4 of Pentecost, Year A**

What then are we to say? Should we continue in sin in order that grace may abound? By no means! How can we who died to sin go on living in it? Do you not know that all of us who have been baptized into Christ Jesus were baptized into his death? Therefore we have been buried with him by baptism into death, so that, just as Christ was raised from the dead by the glory of the Father, so we too might walk in newness of life.

For if we have been united with him in a death like his, we will certainly be united with him in a resurrection like his. We know that our old self was crucified with him so that the body of sin might be destroyed, and we might no longer be enslaved to sin. For whoever has died is freed from sin. But if we have died with Christ, we believe that we will also live with him. We know that Christ, being raised from the dead, will never die again; death no longer has dominion over him. The death he died, he died to sin, once for all; but the life he lives, he lives to God. So you also must consider yourselves dead to sin and alive to God in Christ Jesus.

Comments on the Text

When a person dies, all those who were involved in the life of that person are changed forever. No longer will they be able to enjoy a quiet meal, to share intimate secrets, to bake cookies, or to debate the current

political landscape with the deceased. The reality of this changed existence usually occurs at the time of burial. When the person is entombed,
and family and friends are forced to walk away from the grave, they come
face to face with the stark reality that they are going home alone, never
again to share in that person's life. Paul uses this same burial and death
imagery to demonstrate the forever changed condition of a life "in Christ
Jesus" (6:11).

The rite of baptism has been important for the church from its earliest beginnings, and no less so for Paul.[1] From the various letters we can
attribute directly to Paul, we can surmise a great deal about his theology
and practice of baptism. However, it must also be noted that Paul never
gave a comprehensive, detailed description of the rite of baptism, as he
did with the Lord's supper in 1 Corinthians 11. Therefore, as is true with
the other Pauline baptismal texts, this passage should not be viewed as a
structure, creed, or directive concerning the baptismal ritual. What we
can surmise is that the rite of baptism was universally and consistently
practiced throughout the various Christian communities.

If the actual act of baptism is not the issue for Paul here, then what is?
The issue at the heart of this text is the significance of the act of baptism.
Paul opens his discussion with a rhetorical question: "Should we continue in sin in order that grace may abound?" (6:1). The structure of the
question is such that the reader understands immediately that the question is absurd, and the answer is obviously negative, which Paul points out
in verse 2, "By no means!" Paul means for the question to sound absurd
and ridiculous, in order to use it as a segue to what he really wants to say:
that those who have "been baptized into Christ Jesus were baptized into
his death" (6:3).

The key to unlocking the significance of baptism is found in Paul's
understanding that "we have died to sin" (6:2) and have been "raised from
the dead" (6:4). Death pays the price for sin. For whoever is dead is no
longer a slave to sin, but "is freed from sin" (6:7). If a person is dead, then
he is, among other things, free from the power of sin, for the dead can no
longer rebel against God. This explains the condition of those who have
literally died, but it does not explain how this helps those who are still
living. For the living to be free of sin they must not only die, but they
must rise from death "so that we too might walk in newness of life" (6:4).

Baptism into the "life" of Christ also implies that one is baptized into
the "death" of Jesus. Through baptism a relationship between the believer
and the actual event of God's saving action in Jesus' death is created. We
are "united with him [Jesus] in a death like his" (6:5). This death is a one-
time event; it does not need to be repeated over and over again. Unlike

the mystery cults of the first century C.E., in which the nature-deity dies annually and is raised in a continual renewal of nature, "the historical event to which baptism pointed was a *once* for all, unique event."[2] The death of Christ is a "once and for all" event which frees the believer from sin's ownership. However, Christian baptism does not signal God to begin a relationship with the believer, because God is already in relationship with the believer. Baptism is the event wherein the believer outwardly acknowledges his or her awarness of the relationship. As C. E. B. Cranfield states, baptism

> points to, and is a pledge of, that death which the person con-
> cerned has already died—in God's sight. On God's side, it is the
> sign and pledge that the benefits of Christ's death for all people
> really does apply to this individual in particular while, on
> humanity's side, it is the outward ratification (we are thinking of
> adult baptism here) of the human decision of faith, of the re-
> sponse already begun to what God has done in Christ.[3]

The death represented in baptism is a sign of the change in a person's life, once and forever.

As with the actual death of an individual, the believer's shared death with Jesus constitutes an immediate and permanent change. We are now able to walk away from the grave of our old master, sin, and serve our new master, God. Baptism altered our past—we are no longer the slaves of sin—but baptism also alters our future in that we are raised in Christ and have new life. In our raised state we are called to "walk in newness of life" (6:4). "Walk" is frequently used in the New Testament to denote the way a person conducts his or her life. A moral life of justice and righteousness, a life that is "new" and superior to the old life, can now be led because we also share in Christ's resurrection. Ernst Käsemann explains it in these terms: "the apostle expects our resurrection only in the future and...sees in the new obedience an anticipation of it and the sign of the already present reality of its power."[4] In the risen Christ we too are free to "live to God" (6:10).

In sharing in the death and resurrection of Christ, Christians are able to walk away from their old life and embrace a new life. Paul's concern here is "that we take the place occupied by the earthly Jesus and thus declare the lordship of the exalted One."[5] In baptism we acknowledge what God has done for us in Jesus and commit ourselves to God. We commit ourselves to live our lives as true disciples, serving our living master: God.

Could This Be Paradise?

There once was a man who was very unhappy with his life. Nothing ever seemed to be right. He had to work too hard for too little money. Neither his friends nor his neighbors gave him the respect he felt he deserved. His wife was always complaining, and his children were never satisfied.

No matter how hard he worked or how high he hoped, his condition did not improve, so he spent most of his time dreaming about Paradise. Whether he was alone or with others, whether at work or at rest, the idea of Paradise filled his head. "Someday," he kept telling himself, "someday I'm going to go to Paradise."

And one day—no different from any other—he decided that this was the day he was going to set off for Paradise.

Rising from his morning table, without saying a word to his wife or his two children, he went out the front door, past the gate with the broken latch, and through the open fields, until he came to the edge of the marketplace. Before he entered the market he knew exactly which women would be arguing with which merchants over the price of which goods. He then passed a bakery opposite a butcher shop, went on through the center of town with its synagogue and town hall, and continued walking on through yet another set of fields to the base of a long, steep hill.

He climbed the hill until he reached the beginning of a broad plateau. There he paused and took one last look at his village below. He was sure he would never see it again. He was a man bound for Paradise.

All day he walked along that plateau, and when the sun was setting in the west, he decided to take shelter under a tall pine tree. Now before going to sleep, he removed his shoes and pointed them in the direction he was sure Paradise lay.

But how was he to know that in the darkest hour of the night an imp—either to punish him or to save him or to teach him a lesson or maybe just to play a joke on him—would come by and take his shoes and turn them around? There was no way for the man to know that.

The next morning the man rose early, said his prayers, and stepped into his shoes, certain that they would lead him to Paradise. Off he went heading in the direction his shoes pointed. His head was filled with dreams. Suddenly, there he was at the edge of the plateau, and just below him, Paradise. He had arrived.

Strange, he thought, *Paradise is not much bigger than my own village. Oh, well.*

He descended the hill and walked through the fields to the center of town. Here in Paradise there was also a synagogue and a town hall. As he stood there looking at them, the man thought, *They've been lying to me all these years—or at least exaggerating. They said that everything in Paradise would shine and gleam, but these buildings, why, they're almost as shabby and run-down as the buildings in my own village.*

He passed a bakery that stood opposite a butcher shop. He began to suspect that when he entered the marketplace, he would know which women would buy what goods from which merchants at what price and what they would argue about—and sure enough, he did!

Now he was more sad than angry. He was sure that if he continued through the fields in front of him, he would come to a gate with a broken latch—and he did.

As he stood there pondering his situation, he heard a whining voice from the house. "Come in and eat your food."

It was enough to drive a man mad. It sounded just like his own wife. But never having said no to his wife and being a bit hungry, he decided to go inside the house. Once inside he sat down, ate some black bread and some herring, and drank a cup of coffee.

Two children came running up to him and jumped into his lap. Playing with his long beard, the youngest one asked, "You'll stay with us this time, won't you, Papa?"

Not wanting to say no to the children, the man agreed to stay.

And to this very day, that man sits at that table every morning, drinking his coffee, trying to figure out whether he's in Paradise or not.[6]

Reflections on the Story

Of all the scripture texts a children's sermon giver will ever have to work with, the Pauline and other New Testament letters are the most difficult from which to create children's sermons. Because of their difficulty, the need for good exegetical analysis and a good file of stories, folk tales, and fairy tales becomes critical. In finding a story that will keep the children's interest, and at the same time point out the message of the Pauline text, I found it is necessary to boil the message down to its lowest common denominator. A story would have to have an event that changed the life of the main character from one of "rebellion" to one of "thankfulness."

"Could This Be Paradise?" is a good story that demonstrates the effects of a changed life. The analogies from the story to the text at times are a bit stretched. However, the message of change comes through clearly. In this story the man is unhappy with his life and decides to do something about it. In much the same way that some people come to church for the first time, he decides to seek out paradise. On his journey toward paradise something changes his direction and his life is forever changed. Is he in paradise or not? This is a question that the man struggles with "to this very day." Just as the man must struggle with living in his world, we too must struggle with living in this world. But because of "the glory of God" (6:4) we are able to be "alive to God in Christ Jesus" (6:11).

NOTES

[1] Ernst Käsemann, *Commentary on Romans* (Grand Rapids: William B. Eerdmans Publishing, 1980), p. 164; also see C. E. B. Cranfield, *Romans: A Shorter Commentary* (Grand Rapids: William B. Eerdmans Publishing, 1985), p. 130.

[2] Cranfield, *Romans*, p. 130.

[3] Ibid., p. 131 (altered to be inclusive).

[4] Käsemann, *Commentary on Romans*, p. 167.

[5] Ibid., p. 69.

[6] A Jewish folktale.

16

The Secret Ingredient

Matthew 13:31–33, 44–46   **Week 10 of Pentecost, Year A**

He put before them another parable: "The kingdom of heaven is like a mustard seed that someone took and sowed in his field; it is the smallest of all the seeds, but when it has grown it is the greatest of shrubs and becomes a tree, so that the birds of the air come and make nests in its branches."

He told them another parable: "The kingdom of heaven is like yeast that a woman took and mixed in with three measures of flour until all of it was leavened.

"The kingdom of heaven is like treasure hidden in a field, which someone found and hid; then in his joy he goes and sells all that he has and buys that field.

"Again, the kingdom of heaven is like a merchant in search of fine pearls; on finding one pearl of great value, he went and sold all that he had and bought it."

Comments on the Text

The parables retold by the Gospel writers are both easy and difficult to interpret. As David Barr says: "They speak directly to the reader, but they come to us preceded by a history of interpretations, including those of the Gospel writers."[1] This group of four parables is no different. They are easy, but difficult at the same time. For children, parables can be a wonderful tool to use to help them develop their faith.

On the surface these four parables have no visible connection to one another, other than being in the same parable chapter of Matthew as three other parables. However, as different as they sound, they are directly connected to one another. The first two (the mustard seed and the leaven) emphasize God's action, and the last set (the treasure and the pearl) stress the human response to God's action.

It is important to keep in mind that the Matthew community, like the Mark community, was strongly influenced by an apocalyptic worldview. Both communities were looking forward to the imminent arrival of God's rule. But, unlike the Mark version that uses the parable chapter (Mark 4) to announce the coming of the kingdom of God, the Matthew story has already made the announcement that the kingdom of God is here now, through John the Baptist (3:2). The parables here in chapter 13 serve the purpose of describing the kingdom that is present but not yet completed. Like the mustard seed or leaven that are almost imperceptible in the beginning yet have great growth, the kingdom of God also grows, thus offering encouragement to those living in the in-between time. Douglas Hare describes the parables of the mustard seed and the leaven in these terms:

> Both proclaim that God's action in the world, while almost imperceptible (the mustard seed was proverbial as the smallest thing that an eye could see) or hidden (as leaven in dough), is nonetheless real and will in God's own time come to full fruition. Both assume that the kingdom of God is not a strictly future reality that will suddenly appear full blown without any prior activity. In Jesus' ministry the kingdom has been mysteriously inaugurated.[2]

The two parables invite the hearer to recognize that God is active in the tiniest of movement begun by Jesus. The mustard seed and leaven parables remind the hearer that God is not irrelevant but is present in the everyday, insignificant activity of life, such as baking bread or the growth and nurture of nature.

The parable of the treasure in the field and the pearl are the counterpoints to the mustard seed and leaven, from God's action to human response. Like the leaven, the treasure is also hidden from human eyes. God's activities are hidden and must be "found" or discovered. Likewise, to find a pearl "of great value," one must seek it. Brandon Scott defines the value of the treasure and pearl in these terms:

> Treasure receives its value, its joy, because it appears outside the bounds of the everyday. It is an occurrence that breaks expectation and interrupts the everyday. Because it is not something earned or labored for but something found, it is lawless. Its joy is precisely in its lawlessness, its unearned, not worked for character.[3]

This is the joy of "finding" God's freely given grace of love.

As important as the search may be, the point of the parables is in the response of those who discover the treasure and the fine pearl. In both cases, once the discovery is made the individual "sells all that he has" to possess the discovery. This, however, must not be confused with the notion that the kingdom can somehow be purchased or acquired. Indeed, the treasure and the pearl point out that the kingdom, "treasure hidden" and "a pearl found," comes before our deeds, in which we "sell all that [we] have and buy" (13:44). The first two parables point to the gift of the kingdom of heaven from God. God is at work, although unseen. In the second set of parables the human response to the free gift of the kingdom of heaven is witnessed. The parables instruct us that the human response to the free gift of the kingdom of heaven is to be complete and total, selling all that we have. Or as Douglas Hare concludes: "Those whose eyes have been opened to see what God is doing in Jesus must commit themselves wholeheartedly in faith and obedience."[4]

CHILDREN'S SERMON ────────────────────────

The Secret Ingredient

Early one fall morning, a stranger entered the little village of Luphen. He was as tall and thin as a cedar sapling. His clothes hung on him like rags on a stick. The villagers, who had gathered in the square to watch him, eyed him warily, for they had nothing to spare for a hungry beggar. Their eyes grew as big as soup bowls when he sat down in the middle of the town square and took something out of his pocket. Clenching the mysterious object between both hands, he made slow circular motions in the air with his fists locked together.

An old woman shouted at the stranger, "What are you doing?"

Without looking up, the stranger said, "I'm making my lunch," and he continued to stir the air.

The old woman said, "Lunch! Hunger has made you crazy, man. You're stirring nothing but air."

For the first time the stranger looked up and with a twinkle in eyes said, "Ah, but there soon will be."

The old woman replied, "How?"

The stranger licked his lips and said, "In my hands I hold a magical secret ingredient. It has the power to create the best soup you or anyone has ever tasted."

The old woman said, "This I have to see."

The stranger sighed, "And I would gladly show you if I only had a large pot."

The old woman scratched her head, feeling a light rumble of hunger in her stomach, and said, "A pot, eh? Wait here." She rushed to her cottage and raced back carrying her largest cooking pot.

The stranger sighed again and said, "I will need this pot filled with water so that my magic ingredient will make the most delicious soup you have ever tasted."

Two strong men who were standing nearby hesitated for a moment and then grabbed four buckets, filled them at the well, and emptied them into the pot.

The stranger held both hands over the pot of water. The villagers held their breath. The stranger pulled back his hands and said, "Ah, if only…"

The villagers cried, "If only what?"

The stranger said, "If only I had a fire to heat the water. My secret ingredient only works its magic in hot water."

The children of the village quickly scattered to collect dry wood for the fire. As soon as they returned, a man stepped forward and lit a fire under the pot.

Once the water began to boil, the stranger once again held both hands over the pot. There wasn't a sound to be heard in the village. The stranger raised his head to the heavens and said, "But, but…something is missing."

The villagers looked to the heavens, then to the stranger and cried, "What…what could be missing?"

The stranger said, "Vegatables, if only I had a vegetable or two to add to my secret ingredient. Then the soup would taste heavenly."

Six women darted home and quickly brought back handfuls of carrots, celery, onions, and potatoes. The stranger watched as the vegetables were dumped into the pot. Once again he held his hands over the pot and again he drew them back quickly. "I can't" is all he said.

The villagers exclaimed, "Why not?"

The stranger said, "There is one more thing that would make the soup so rich that the king himself, were he to taste it, would be envious."

The villagers cried, "Tell us! Tell us!"

He said sadly, shaking his head, "I think…no, never mind."

No one spoke. Then suddenly a small voice broke the silence and asked, "Ham?"

"Yes, ham," the stranger replied.

No sooner was this said than an old woman hurried home and returned with a small ham. She dropped it into the steaming pot. Soon a wonderful smell filled the air, and the villagers began to shout, "Put your secret ingredient in *now!*"

The stranger smiled and said, "Gladly."

He then held his clenched fists over the bubbling pot and dramatically opened them. The villagers gasped as they watched a tiny pebble fall from the man's hands and plop into the soup.

"A pebble is the secret ingredient!" they cried.

The stranger replied, "But wait until you taste the soup."

After the villagers had filled their bowls and hungrily ate all of the soup, they said to the stranger, "Yes, this was a soup fit for a king. And to think a pebble made it so delicious."

But the stranger said, "Not just any pebble, but a rare magic soup pebble. And because you have been so kind to me, I will leave this one with you so you will always be able to make such wonderful soup."

With that the stranger said farewell. As he began walking toward the next village, the people of Luphen did not see that one of his pockets sagged from the weight of pebbles.[5]

Reflections on the Story

Magic or mystery is something that all children relate to. At their present stage of development, wonder and amazement are found in the most common events. Magic is a part of their lives and who they are. It is only when we "mature" that magic/mystery must be explained and reasoned out. Because of their mysterious/magical nature, these four parables can be particularly fun for children, especially if a story can be found that contains the idea of a small "mysterious" or "magical" ingredient that makes the common everyday, uncommon and special.

"The Secret Ingredient" brings to life the mystery of the leaven and the mustard seed. The pebble that will produce a soup fit for the king is small, and in the visitor's hands it is virtually imperceptible. But, when the pebble is added to the soup at just the right moment—magically it transforms the soup into something special. Most intriguing, and what the children will notice, is that the magic is not in what the pebble does, but what happens when the people come together. Like the merchant and the field buyer, the people bring out and add to the soup all that they have: a pot, vegetables, a ham. In giving all they had, they discovered that they had finally given to each other and were part of something bigger.

NOTES

[1] David L. Barr, *New Testament Story: An Introduction* (Belmont, California: Wadsworth Publishing, 1987), p. 193.

[2] Douglas R. A. Hare, *Matthew* (Louisville: John Knox Press, 1993), p. 156.

[3] Bernard Brandon Scott, *Hear Then the Parable: A Commentary on the Parables of Jesus* (Minneapolis: Fortress Press, 1989), p. 401f.

[4] Hare, *Matthew*, p. 158.

[5] A Russian folktale.

17

How Men and Women Finally Agreed

Luke 14:25–33   **Week 16 of Pentecost, Year C**

Now large crowds were traveling with him; and he turned and said to them, "Whoever comes to me and does not hate father and mother, wife and children, brother and sisters, yes, and even life itself, cannot be my disciple. Whoever does not carry the cross and follow me cannot be my disciple. For which of you, intending to build a tower, does not first sit down and estimate the cost, to see whether he has enough to complete it? Otherwise, when he has laid a foundation and is not able to finish, all who see it will begin to ridicule him, saying, 'This fellow began to build and was not able to finish.' Or what king, going out to wage war against another king, will not sit down first and consider whether he is able with ten thousand to oppose the one who comes against him with twenty thousand? If he cannot, then, while the other is still far away, he sends a delegation and asks for the terms of peace. So therefore, none of you can become my disciples if you do not give up all your possessions.

Comments on the Text

I spent fifteen years in retail sales and management. In that time I discovered one truism: People always ask the price of something when they need to buy it, but when they desire to have something, they never ask the price. When we desire something, the price becomes unimportant,

128

and all too often we discover much later that the cost was too high. As Christians, we, too, fall into this dilemma. Joining a fellowship with great enthusiasm and high hopes for a better life, few take into consideration the consequences of their decision. In this story, Jesus asks the large crowds following him, as well as ourselves, "Do you understand what following me costs?"

The storyteller suddenly turns from the stationary teaching setting of a Pharisee's house in 14:1–24 to the journey motif that dominates Luke's Gospel in verse 25. This sudden shift in placement and setting informs the reader that what is to follow is addressed to a different audience. The preceding story is addressed to those who have already made the decision to follow Jesus.[1] "Large crowds were traveling with him" (14:25). These people came to him (14:26); Jesus did not call them into a life of discipleship. Unlike a charlatan or sideshow huckster who lures the unsuspecting with promises of an easy life and quick riches, Jesus intentionally asks those who are following to stop and consider the demands and consequences of what their decision will require. Discipleship is not easy and should not be entered into lightly is the warning.

The storyteller has Jesus ask the followers to consider the cost of discipleship by using a series of literary constructs called an *inclusio*. Each series of questions or considerations is built on the phrase "Whoever does not...cannot be my disciple" (14:26, 27, 33). The inclusio is a typical literary device used by storytellers to combine sayings that otherwise do not belong together into a single unit that then acts as a set of conditions.[2] In the first of these questions Jesus asks his followers to "hate father and mother, wife and children, brother and sister, yes, and even life itself" (14:26). There are a few passages, verses, and phrases in the Bible that everyone wishes were not in it, or that they would like to ignore and pretend were not there, and this is one of them. Jesus, of all people, the one who has taught nothing but love, now asks us to hate those whom we should love the most. However, what we have here is a perfect example of how limited the English language can be in translating the original Greek text, especially if the Greek is an attempt to translate a Semitic expression. In English we have but one word for hate and with it all the vicious, emotionally charged connotations. However, the Greek verb for "to hate" does not mean intense feelings of hostility and anger; it indicates a set of conditions. If there is a conflict between discipleship and one's relationship with one's mother, then discipleship is to take precedence. This may reflect an earlier Semitic meaning of turning away from or detachment from.[3] Thus, when the claims of Christ are placed upon a person, that person is called to put Christ first above all others, even those whom she or he is the closest to. The cost of discipleship is not cheap; it demands the transformation of relationships.

There are two parables placed in between the second and third conditions. These two parables have no parallels in the other Gospel stories, and are simple observations that prudent persons don't undertake a project until they have assessed the cost and are sure they can finish it. The first parable comes from rural life. The building of a tower on farm land sounds strange today; however, towers where a regular and common farm structure in the days of Jesus. The tower was built as a lookout so that the farmer could watch for thieves and scavenging animals. No farmer would build a tower, a major financial investment, unless he was sure he had enough funds to complete its construction. The second parable is a story of a royal house where decisions of war and peace are made. The decision to fight or negotiate peace was not a simple choice, and more was at stake than the loss of soliders. Thus, no king undertook war without first considering the cost of soliders, land, sovereignty, and pride. The two parables demonstrate vividly that, regardless of whether one is rich or poor, peasant or noble, everyone must make the same decision when faced with a major expenditure: "Does it cost more than I am able or willing to pay?"[4] And this is the question that Jesus put to the large crowds who traveled with him and asks of us still today, "Are you ready, able, and willing to pay the cost of true discipleship?"

Following the two parables the storyteller returns to the third and final inclusio condition. This final condition of discipleship is a stern warning to not only those who wish to follow Jesus, but to those who have been following. The first two inclusios are addressed specifically to those seeking to follow, but here all who have been following are included in a reminder of what is still required and how high the price really is. This idea is more clearly understood in the Greek. The verb translated to "give up" (14:33), is from a Greek verb that literally means "to say farewell to" or "to take leave of."[5] This condition of discipleship to say farewell to all of your possessions also returns the Luke storyteller to a favorite Lukan theme—a predisposition for the poor, and giving and caring for the poor.

Life is not easy; the cost of everything we do is high, whether it is building a house or buying a lawn mower. We would never expect people to blindly do whatever they wish without thinking through the consequences. As a matter of fact, we tend to be like the neighbors of the farmer and "begin to ridicule" those who impulsively set out without considering the cost (14:29). Yet, when it comes to our religion we are guilty at times of building a foundation in our enthusiasm without the ability to complete the tower.

CHILDREN'S SERMON ━━━━━━━━━━━━━━━━━━━━━━━━

How Men and Women Finally Agreed

L ong ago when the world was new the Creator made a man named Kikuyu. The Creator taught Kikuyu how to farm and raise animals and, most importantly, how to care for the land. After Kikuyu had learned all there was to learn, the Creator took Kikuyu to the top of the Bright Mountain and pointed far off in the distance.

"Do you see that plot of land in the middle of the world—where the fig trees stand? Go there and make your home. When you arrive there you will find a wife. Go now and may your life and the lives of your children be happy."

So Kikuyu walked to the middle of the world. The figs were large and juicy, deep and dark. But they were not the best things about the grove of fig trees in the middle of the world. For when Kikuyu arrived he found waiting for him a beautiful wife, Moombi, and nine lovely daughters.

For a long time Kikuyu and his family lived happily, farming, raising animals, and caring for the land just as the Creator had taught him. But as time passed and he saw the birds sing their love songs and watched the sheep lambing in the fields, he began to wonder if his daughters would ever be able to marry and have children of their own to make them as happy as they made Kikuyu and Moombi.

So one day the whole family left the grove of fig trees in the middle of the world and made the long walk to the Bright Mountain to ask the Creator's advice.

"I would like to hear the sound of men's voices in my fields, and my daughters would love to see the faces of men coming home from the fields at night," Kikuyu told the Creator. "What then should I do to have sons-in-law?"

"Go home, Kikuyu. Go home. But always remember that the name of Kikuyu is precious to me, but the name of Moombi is sacred."

Puzzled by the Creator's answer, but ever obedient, Kikuyu did as he was told and returned to the grove of fig trees in the middle of the world with his family.

To their surprise and amazement, there in the middle of the fields stood nine young men.

"Oh, papa!" cried the girls, "Aren't they beautiful!"

Kikuyu thought for a moment about the words the Creator had spoken, and then said to the young men, "Is marriage agreeable to you?"

"Yes, sir!"

"And marriage is agreeable to you, my daughters?"

"Yes, oh yes, Papa!"

"And you, my wife, is the marriage between these young men and our daughters agreeable to you?"

"It is time, and none too soon!" laughed Moombi.

"Then, it is agreed," declared Kikuyu. "But on one condition, you must take the name of Moombi for your family name and obey your wives in all things."

The young men agreed, and their marriages were long and happy. And so it was that whenever a couple died, their hut and hoe and inheritance passed from daughter to daughter. The daughters chose whom they would marry, and all lived happily, and the Moombi grew into a tribe.

After many generations, the men grew disgruntled. One hated doing all the washing. One resented his wife, who beat him when the sheep got loose in the garden. Another felt sorry for his sons because they would never inherit anything. So the men muttered and mumbled together and began to plot how they could end their wives' mastery over them. But how could they do it? The women fought better, ran faster, cursed louder, and thought quicker than the men.

So they waited and waited until one day when all the women were expecting babies. They waited until the wives were as big as hippopotamuses and waddled around like ducks.

"*We* want to be in charge now," the men declared one day. And because the women were so big, they could do nothing about the change. The men began to make the wives do all the washing and cooking, while the men sat in council all day passing laws that favored men.

Then it happened, the unthinkable. "Wives!" they said. "We have decided that we will no longer take your name as our family name. From now on it will be the woman who takes a male's name. And no longer will the tribe be called Moombi Kikuyu, named after a woman, but we will be the…"

"Enough!" shouted an elder woman. She stood up to her full height and squared her shoulders and said, "If that is the case, then we shall bear you no more sons. For the name of Kikuyu is precious in the ear of God, but the name of Moombi is sacred. If you do this thing, we who are pregnant will only give birth to daughters, and after that we will bear you no children at all! If you ever wish to have a son, from now on, give birth to them yourselves."

The other women began to laugh and nod in agreement, while the men looked down at their narrow hips and thought about the possibility of bearing a son. "No, the privilege of bearing children we will leave to you," they said.

And so it is that to this day the daughters are called Moombi. And as for the sons...why they are called Moombi of course.[6]

Reflections on the Story

This story is quite odd for most contemporary Americans. The story evolves around the direct opposite of our social and cultural norm of patriarchal supremacy. This is one reason that I have chosen this particular story. Like most of the parables of Jesus, this story flies in the face of what we think is right and proper. By doing so it jolts us into thinking about the truth contained in the story, and not about what is socially acceptable or culturally required.

The story reminds us all that regardless of what we may want, regardless of what we may perceive as right, if we blindly walk in and just take what we want without thinking through the consequences, we may find that we have bitten off more than we can chew. The early Christians understood that the cost of discipleship was and still is high. Many risked their status, their livelihood, and even their lives when they literally gave up all they possessed (Acts 2:44; 4:32). Contemporary North American Christianity, however, often finds itself focused on trying to overturn the system, like the men of Moombi. Instead of advising new or potential members of the cost and commitment required in being a Christian, we offer the no commitment "grace guarantee," pretending not to know the costs involved. The men of Moombi discovered that the cost of male dominance was too high a price to pay, but not until they learned the hard way by plunging in head first. The question then becomes, are we going to follow Jesus' way of being honest on the front side, or not?

NOTES

[1] Fred B. Craddock, *Luke* (Louisville: John Knox Press, 1990), p. 180; also see R. Alan Culpepper, "The Gospel of Luke," *The New Interpreter's Bible*, vol. 9 (Nashville: Abingdon Press, 1995), p. 292.

[2] Craddock, *Luke*, p. 181.

[3] Eduard Schweizer, *The Good News According to Luke*, translated by David E. Green (Atlanta: John Knox Press, 1984), p. 241; also see Craddock, *Luke*, p. 182.

[4] Craddock, *Luke*, p. 182.

[5] Culpepper, "The Gospel of Luke," p. 293.

[6] A Moombi-Kikuyu African folktale.

18

The Honest Shepherd

Matthew 22:1–14   Week 20 of Pentecost, Year A

Once more Jesus spoke to them in parables, saying: "The kingdom of heaven may be compared to a king who gave a wedding banquet for his son. He sent his slaves to call those who had been invited to the wedding banquet, but they would not come. Again he sent other slaves, saying, 'Tell those who have been invited: Look, I have prepared my dinner, my oxen and my fat calves have been slaughtered, and everything is ready; come to the wedding banquet.' But they made light of it and went away, one to his farm, another to his business, while the rest seized his slaves, mistreated them, and killed them. The king was enraged. He sent his troops, destroyed those murderers, and burned their city. Then he said to his slaves, 'The wedding is ready, but those invited were not worthy. Go therefore into the main streets, and invite everyone you find to the wedding banquet.' Those slaves went out into the streets and gathered all whom they found, both good and bad; so the wedding hall was filled with guests.

"But when the king came in to see the guests, he noticed a man there who was not wearing a wedding robe, and he said to him, 'Friend, how did you get in here without a wedding robe?' And he was speechless. Then the king said to the attendants, 'Bind him hand and foot, and throw him into the outer darkness, where there will be weeping and gnashing of teeth.' For many are called, but few are chosen."

Comments on the Text

When my wife and I are invited to a party, the first thing she always asks is, "What are we supposed to wear?" An invitation requires a response from those who have been invited. The two parables—the feast parable, 22:1–10, and the wedding garment parable, 22:11–14, known together as the wedding feast parable—present Christians with an invitation to the kingdom of God and the appropriate response to that invitation.

As we approach these two parables in one, it may be helpful to review the structure of the Matthean text. Matthew can be divided into four sections: the revelation of who is Jesus Christ (1–10); the responses of various groups to Jesus (11–17); the response of Jesus to various groups (18–25); and the righteousness of Jesus vindicated (26–28).[1] The wedding feast parable is the third in a series of parables in which Jesus responds to challenges concerning his authority.[2] These three parables are not only a response to Jesus' authority but display a major theological theme in Matthew: The church is the true Israel.[3]

This parable, as well as other judgment parables in Matthew (particularly 25:31–46), is a judgment on "those invited [but who] were not worthy" (22:8), or in other words the "False Israel." But the parables also have an individual interpretation as judgment on "both good and bad" (25:10). This understanding of the wedding feast parable is clearly seen in the two characteristics of Jesus promoted by the Matthean author: "Jesus is one endowed with great authority, and conversely, he is the supremely obedient one."[4] The wedding feast parable differentiates between what constitutes true and false discipleship and is not necessarily a judgment on any particular group or faction. If we keep these two Matthean characteristics in mind and couple it with the Pauline imperative to "be imitators of God" (Eph. 5:1), the parable becomes an invitation for all to God's divine grace and our human response to God's invitation.

The wedding feast parable can be classified as an allegory of salvation history. The king represents God; the wedding feast for the king's son, the messianic banquet (Revelation 19:7–9); the servants or slaves represent God's prophets and apostles/Christian missionaries. It is important to note here that within this parabolic text there are definite clues that Matthew was written after the destruction of Jerusalem by Rome that concluded the Judean Rebellion (70 C.E.). The reference at verse 7 to the king who sent troops who "destroyed those murderers, and burned their city" directly indicates the destruction of Jerusalem. This event was regarded by early Christians as God's punishment on Israel for rejecting Jesus and the gospel. The destruction of the city "signifies the final turning away from Israel and toward the Gentiles."[5] However, in reconstructing the allegorical connections, the invitation to "both good and bad" (verse 10) represents God's unconditional love for all humanity, Jew and Gentile alike.

The judgment in the first parable is clear—rejection of God's invitation to the feast invites death and destruction. Equally clear is that Matthew points out that this judgment is not reserved for only the Jews, but for the church itself, "both good and bad."[6] It can also be argued that this is the meaning behind the attached saying at verse 14, "for many are called, but few are chosen."

The second parable, the wedding garment, is offensive to most readers. Jesus, the person who taught us to love our neighbors, to care for the sick, the destitute, the lame, the widow, and the orphan, here tells a story of a poor person being thrown "into the outer darkness, where there will be weeping and gnashing of teeth" (verse 13). This poor person is treated in this manner simply because he is not wearing the proper clothing. The parable on the surface appears to stand in stark contrast to the loving, compassionate Jesus of the rest of the Gospel narrative. The answer is found in remembering this is not just a story, but it is an allegory story.[7] The wedding feast is not the church but God's kingdom, and the wedding robe is the way one is to live one's life in accordance with Jesus' teaching. The invitation to the feast requires a change in living. One cannot simply hear the invitation of the gospel; one must live out the gospel directives.

CHILDREN'S SERMON ━━━━━━━━━━━━━━━━━━━━━━━━━━━━

The Honest Shepherd

Once upon a time there lived a woman with her two sons. The older boy was lazy and greedy, but the youngest was kind and hardworking. One day when the poor widow had almost run out of food, she sent her oldest son into the world for help.

The boy set off mumbling and grumbling about having to go to work. Before long, he came upon an old shepherd. "Where are you heading?" the old man asked.

"I'm looking for work so I might help my family," the boy complained.

"If you'll care for my sheep, I'll pay you well," the old man said. "All you have to do is take along this little box and this little bottle. And fill them with some of the grass that my sheep have eaten and a little bit of the water they have drunk."

"I can do that," the boy said.

"One more thing," the shepherd szpaid. "You must always follow the sheep wherever they go."

Early the next morning, the older son stood in the pasture watching the flock of sheep graze. After a while, the sheep walked toward the hills. So the boy reluctantly followed. As he followed the sheep, a little snowy lamb affectionately rubbed his leg. But the boy roughly pushed him away. "Go away!" he shouted, and the lamb ran to follow the other sheep.

Before long the flock came to a steep ravine with a rickety, narrow bridge. The sheep began to cross the bridge over the ravine. But when the boy saw how rickety and narrow the bridge was, he shook his head and said, "I won't cross such a dangerous bridge."

The snowy lamb turned to help him across, but the boy crossly said, "Go away!" And so he decided to wait for the sheep until they returned. As the last sheep crossed the bridge, the boy lay down on the grass and fell fast asleep. When he woke, the sheep were returning over the bridge. The boy quickly tore some grass from the patch where he had slept and stuffed it in the box. Then he filled his bottle with water from a nearby spring.

When the boy presented the box and bottle to the old shepherd, the man shook his head. "This is not what my sheep have been eating and drinking," he said. "I'm afraid I'll no longer be needing your help."

"And what about my earnings?" the boy asked indignantly.

"Would you prefer a bag of gold or an honest heart?" the shepherd asked.

The boy laughed, "Give me the gold." So the old man handed him a bag of gold. And the boy set off for home, pleased with his fortune.

That night he decided to stop at a roadside inn to sleep rather than hurry on home. When he woke the next morning, his gold was gone. And so the boy returned to his mother empty-handed.

"Mother," the youngest son said, "I'll go into the world and seek our fortune." Though the mother hated to see her kind child go, she sent him into the world.

As the youngest son was walking, he, too, was met by the old shepherd. The shepherd offered him the same job he had given to his older brother. The boy happily agreed to give it a try.

Now, the younger son was a very different boy from his brother. So when the little lamb rubbed against his leg, the boy stroked his wool. And when they came to the rickety bridge, he decided to follow the sheep across. The little lamb spoke to the boy. "Hold onto me, little shepherd, and I'll take you safely across."

The boy did as he was told and walked across the bridge and followed the sheep through a dense forest. Soon they came to a land that seemed magical to the boy. There were trees of every shape and size, and from their branches hung the most beautiful fruit the boy had ever seen. Streams of silver flowed through the land. Birds flew everywhere, singing beautiful songs.

Then the most amazing thing happened. The moment the sheep drank from the silver stream, they were transformed into fairies. They pranced around all day, eating fruit, singing songs, and riding on the backs of the birds. As twilight fell, the fairies became sheep once more and began to head for home with the little shepherd following.

When the old shepherd asked the boy for the box and the bottle, the boy handed him a bottle filled with the silvery water and the box filled with fruit.

The old man smiled. "Dear boy, you have done your job well, and I want you to work for me forever. Now you must choose your reward—a bag of gold or an honest heart."

"Oh," said the boy, "my mother is very poor, and we need gold a great deal. But an honest heart is worth more than all the gold in the world. And I must tell you honestly, good sir, your sheep really aren't sheep at all, they are fairies!"

"So they are," said the old shepherd, laughing. And once again the sheep turned into fairies. Each one came and handed the boy a bag of gold. "An honest heart is worth more than all the gold in the world," they each repeated.

The boy hurried home and gave his mother the gold. "And better still," he told her, "I have a job with the old shepherd forever."

"And what about your brother?" his mother asked. "What will he do?"

"He will take care of the chores at home," the young boy said.

From that day on, the older boy changed his ways, for he had learned that an honest heart is a valuable gift.[8]

Reflections on the Story

Finding a story to highlight the point of another story can be difficult. However, when the perfect story is found, the rewards are great. In searching for a story for this scripture text, I laid out several principles that a story would have to contain that speak of our human need to respond appropriately to God's invitation to fellowship. The first principle is to find a story that contains some kind of invitation, not necessarily to a feast or a party but an invitation to a better life. Second, the story must contain judgment and reward. Judgment for choosing the "wrong" way of living and reward for "right" living. Third, the main or principal character of the story lives and follows the "right way" because it is the right way to live and does not live "right" for the pursuit of reward. Finally, the invitation needs to be extended to any and all, regardless of character (bad and good) because of the loving heart of the host.

The story of the Honest Shepherd fits these conditions. A kind-hearted shepherd invites both the lazy older brother and the hardworking younger brother to lifelong employment. Because the older brother chooses to do the job only halfway he is fired and sent away. The older brother's greed also demonstrates that he heard the invitation of the shepherd because he only sought a great reward. The greatness of the reward, however, was not enough to cause the older brother to change his life and respond accordingly to the invitation of the shepherd. The younger brother, on the other hand, by choosing not to accept payment for watching over fairies who needed no watching over, demonstrates the right way to live. This is further demonstrated when he chose as his reward an honest heart over a bag of gold. A loving invitation of security is offered by the shepherd, but only one brother chooses to respond positively to the invitation.

NOTES

[1] David L. Barr, *New Testament Story: An Introduction* (Belmont, California: Wadsworth Publishing, 1987), p. 181.

[2] Douglas R. A. Hare, *Matthew* (Louisville: John Knox Press, 1993), p. 251, and Myra B. Nagel, "Many Called, Few Chosen" in *The Inviting Word* (Cleveland: United Church Press, 1996), p. 61.

[3] Bernard Brandon Scott, *Hear Then the Parable: A Commentary on the Parables of Jesus* (Minneapolis: Fortress Press, 1989), p. 162.

[4] Barr, *New Testament Story*, p. 198.

[5] Scott, *Hear Then the Parable*, p. 163.

[6] Hare, *Matthew*, p. 252.

[7] Ibid.

[8] A Hungarian folktale.

19

The First Bard
Among the Soninke

1 Thessalonians 2:9–12   Week 23 of Pentecost, Year A

You remember our labor and toil, brothers and sisters; we worked night and day, so that we might not burden any of you while we proclaimed to you the gospel of God. You are witnesses, and God also, how pure, upright, and blameless our conduct was toward you believers. As you know, we dealt with each one of you like a father with his children, urging and encouraging you and pleading that you lead a life worthy of God, who calls you into his own kingdom and glory.

Comments on the Text

In contemporary North American society, work is something that people do so they can enjoy their leisure time. In antiquity, work was a sunup to sundown, and then some, activity. If one did not work, one did not eat. Work also was a family affair. Every family member, no matter how young or how old, participated in the work that meant the family would survive. This concept of work is almost impossible for contemporary Americans to understand, yet this is the model that Paul puts forth in 1 Thessalonians 2:9–12.

If work is at issue here, the next logical question must be, "What work?" The Greek word used by Paul does not connote the specific type of work performed by Paul but does imply some form of manual labor.[1]

142 I Love to Tell the Story

The "labor and toil" that the Thessalonians "remember" Paul and his com-
panions doing was not just the typical work from sunrise to sunset; they
began their work before sunrise and continued to work throughout the
day, "night and day" (2:9). However, "Paul's language does not suggest that
he stopped working in order to proclaim the gospel. He proclaimed the
gospel as he worked. The workers put in a long day. While they did so,
they proclaimed the gospel of God."[2]

There is considerable argument among scholars as to why Paul would
remind the Thessalonians of his manual labor while he was with them.
One thought is that Paul was following the rabbinic tradition of manual
labor for rabbis. But, if Paul is writing to a Gentile congregation, this
tradition would be meaningless. Another possibility is that Paul worked
so as not to be a "burden" on the Thessalonians, so he would not be
dependent upon a patron. However, being self-sufficient, at least during
his Thessalonian visit, does not seem to be Paul's aim. Paul was not totally
self-sufficient while in Thessalonica, as he wrote to thank the Philippian
congregation for their "help for my needs" while he was in Thessalonica
(Phil. 4:16). Raymond Collins notes, "Although Paul wanted to enjoy
economic self-sufficiency, it is not at all clear that he looked upon his
tiresome efforts as truly ennobling. Rather he appears to have regarded
his manual labor as a burden to be borne for the sake of the gospel."[3] The
life Paul led, the work he did, and the gospel he preached cannot be
separated from one another: "His life verified his gospel."[4]

The gospel preached and the life led is then one of giving to others.
Paul's reference to his manual labor is a demonstration of Paul's own
willingness to sacrifice and give up his own social status in order to identify with others of lower status, for he did not belong to the working class
and need not "work night and day."[5] However, we must be cautioned not
to view this sacrifice as a heroic gesture on Paul's part. Paul's demonstration of self-giving is "not based on a moral freedom gained by reason and
exercise of the will. It was given by God" (2:1-5).[6] Paul chooses to use
images that reveal his caring and that will in turn lead his "children" to "a
life worthy of God, who calls [them] into his own kingdom and glory"
(2:12).

Not only does Paul show his care for the Thessalonians by his work;
he demonstrates his care for them as "a father with his children" (2:11).
Paul reminds his readers that he "has paid attention to each one of them
and that he has adopted different modes of persuasion: exhortation, con-
solation [NRSV: urging and encouraging], and insistence [NRSV: plead-
ing] (2:12), just as a father pays attention to each of his children."[7] Paul's
description of himself as "father" and the Thessalonian congregation as

"his children," "establishes the manner in which he wishes the relationship to be understood—as one formed by shared experiences that had inextricably linked their lives."[8]

Paul is not establishing a model of continuous or strenuous labor for the Thessalonians, or for contemporary Christians, to imitate. What Paul is establishing is a model of confidence in self-giving. Giving that is worked at "night and day."

CHILDREN'S SERMON ━━━━━━━━━━━━━━━━━━━━━━━━━

The First Bard Among the Soninke

Long ago there were two brothers who left their village to hunt in the bush. Because it was the dry season, they had to travel many days to find the game that had migrated south. But no matter how far they went, they could not find any game to kill. One week they hunted, two weeks they hunted, three weeks, and still they could find nothing; not even the warthogs could be found.

The older brother decided that it was time to return to their village. But because they had traveled so far, they did not know how to return to their village. They searched and searched but could not find the trail that would lead them home. Soon the food they had brought with them ran out. Remember, it was the dry season. In the dry season there was not even fruit for the two boys to eat, and because they could not find any game, they had nothing to eat.

Hunger overtook them.

The days dragged on and the hunger grew worse, until one day the younger brother said, "Brother, I cannot go any farther. I am too hungry. I have no strength to go on. If I am to die, I will die here."

The older brother answered, "I do not want you to die. Rest here while I go on ahead and try to find a small rabbit or something. Wait here, I'll be right back."

The older brother searched high and low, in bushes and trees. But not even a mouse did he find. There was no game of any kind.

"What am I to do?" the eldest wondered. "I cannot let my brother die."

In America, if we were the eldest brother, we might have bought him a hot dog at the store or done something else. But in ancient times they had no stores to buy food, and the brother did the only thing that he knew to do. He took out his knife and cut a piece of meat from his thigh and then returned to where his younger brother was waiting.

Shouting to his younger brother he said, "Look! I have found a small animal and killed it. Wait a moment longer while I cook it and then you will feel healthy and strong again."

So the older brother made a fire and roasted the piece of meat over the flames. After the younger brother ate the meat, his strength immediately returned.

The older brother then saw smoke rising in the distance and knew there must be a village up ahead. He said, "Brother, do you see the smoke? It is a village! We are saved! Wait here and I will go ahead to make sure; then I'll come back for you."

The younger brother answered, "No, I will go with you."

And off they went in the direction of the smoke. So that his brother would not know how he had obtained the piece of meat, the older brother tried to keep his bloody thigh covered as best he could. But blood slowly stained his clothing. When the younger brother saw the blood-stained cloth, he asked, "You are hurt? What happened to you? Were you attacked by a lion or leopard?"

But when he uncovered the older brother's wound, he understood everything.

"Brother," the youngest said, with tears of love streaming down his face, "you have saved my life by sacrificing yourself. There is no greater expression of love than this. Henceforth, I will be your bard and sing of your great deeds and of the history of your family. I will be your servant until the end of time and sing the praises of your noble character."

And so the younger brother became the first bard, and ever since that day it has been the custom for noble families to have bards to tell the stories.[9]

Reflections on the Story

Paul exhorts his new converts in Thessalonica to be imitators of him. To follow his lead as caregivers who love like a father "urging and encouraging" and "pleading," and as caregivers who labor and toil "night and day." Giving of oneself is, as the younger brother states, "the greatest expression of love." A story for this text needs two important elements: care freely and unconditionally given and received, and care given not for the moment but forever.

"The First Bard" offers a story of self-giving. The story offers two sides of self-giving. The first is the "fatherly" love offered by the older brother, who willingly risks his own life by literally giving a piece of himself to his younger brother. The care given by the older brother extends beyond just giving his own flesh but is also found in his willingness to allow his younger brother to rest while he continues to seek help.

The second offer of self-giving may be lost on most of the children who hear this story, as well as the adults, but it is there nonetheless and needs to be noted. The younger brother's offer of servitude as a bard is not just a measure of gratitude. In tribal societies the bard, storyteller, or history keeper is revered and honored, because they "tell" the people who they are and what their history is. The offer to keep the family history is a sign of the younger brother's caring. The younger brother gives of himself to retell the stories of the people "until the end of time."

NOTES

[1] Raymond F. Collins, *The Birth of the New Testament: The Origin and Development of the First Christian Generation* (New York: Crossroad, 1993), p. 12.

[2] Ibid.

[3] Ibid., p. 13.

[4] Abraham J. Malherbe, *Paul and the Thessalonians: The Philosophic Tradition of Pastoral Care* (Philadelphia: Fortress Press, 1987), p. 54.

[5] Ibid., p. 55.

[6] Ibid., p. 59.

[7] Ibid., p. 57.

[8] Ibid., p. 74.

[9] A Soninke African tribal folktale.

20

The Truthful Peasant

Joshua 24:1–3a, 14–15   **Week 24 of Pentecost, Year A**

Then Joshua gathered all the tribes of Israel to Shechem, and summoned the elders, the heads, the judges, and the officers of Israel; and they presented themselves before God. And Joshua said to all the people, "Thus says the LORD, the God of Israel: Long ago your ancestors—Terah and his sons Abraham and Nahor—lived beyond the Euphrates and served other gods. Then I took your father Abraham from beyond the River and led him through all the land of Canaan and made his offspring many.

"Now therefore revere the LORD, and serve him in sincerity and in faithfulness; put away the gods that your ancestors served beyond the River and in Egypt, and serve the LORD. Now if you are unwilling to serve the LORD, choose this day whom you will serve, whether the gods your ancestors served in the region beyond the River or the gods of the Amorites in whose land you are living; but as for me and my household, we will serve the LORD."

Comments on the Text

Virtually from the moment we are born we are taught to keep our promises. At the same time we are being taught this important lesson we begin to expect others to keep their promises that they make to us. Promise keeping is an important part of who we are as human beings. Promise

146

keeping is the measuring stick by which we are judged as being honest or not, trustworthy or not. As children grow they discover that there are conditions, directives, and requirements placed on the promises that they make. Very quickly they learn that how much one will benefit from a promise made is dependent on how well one meets the various conditions, directives, and requirements of the promise. In the Shechem covenant story (Joshua 24:1–28) we come face to face with one of the first recorded promises of God's people to God.

There is one predominant theme throughout the book of Joshua: God's faithfulness to the promises as described in the Pentateuch, the first five books of the Old Testament, made to the children of Israel.[1] This point is made clear in the Shechem covenant story. Verses 3–13 recount all the promises made and kept by God to the Israelites (21:3–13). The covenant underlines the importance of God's faithful commitment to the promises. Step by step "all the tribes of Israel" (24:1) are reminded of each promise made and unconditionally kept by God.[2] In the first half of the Shechem covenant God does not place conditions on God's promises but keeps God's end of the bargain out of love.

The second half of the Shechem covenant can be viewed in one of two ways. The first way to view verses 14–24 is as a list of conditions, directives, and requirements that people are to keep to guarantee God's future faithful commitment to the promises.[3] This interpretation is evident in verse 20: "If you forsake the LORD and serve foreign gods, then he will turn and do you harm, and consume you, after having done you good." With the stroke of a pen the writers of Joshua change the promise from an unconditional act of love dependent on God into a conditional act that depends on humanity. However, another possible interpretation seems to be more appropriate. Because God has been faithful to the promises, the people should also be faithful to the promises. This interpretation makes sense when we examine the implications of a historical understanding of treaties and covenants.

Covenants and treaties specified who was the overlord and who was the subject and what each was responsible for. The overlord of this covenant is God, whom the Israelites "presented themselves before" (24:1). The subjects of the covenant are the Israelites. There is one important difference between the Shechem covenant and that of other covenants from antiquity: whom the people owed fidelity to. As Anthony Ceresko notes:

> They owed allegiance to no human sovereign. Their destiny, their future, was not in the hands of one or another human being, but in the sovereign care of their covenant God. In other words, within

the context of obedience to the covenant stipulations, they were in effect free to determine their own conduct and control their own history.[4]

The conditions, directives, and requirements placed on the Israelites in verses 14–24 are not to guarantee God's faithfulness to the promises but are there to remind the people to be faithful to their promise to God. While God is and continues to be faithful to the covenants made to Israel, it is humanity that tends to break those same covenants, causing themselves to be harmed and consumed. Therefore, the children of Israel are asked to make a decision to either continue breaking the covenant and follow "foreign gods" or keep the covenant with God and "serve the Lord" (24:21).

Joshua's role in the Shechem covenant should not be overlooked. He was considered a great leader, the successor of Moses. However, it is not the person Joshua that is important here but the knowledge of what made a leader great or legendary. A person did not become great because of his superior leadership skills or military prowess. What made Joshua and other legendary leaders great was their faithfulness "as servant[s] of the Lord" (24:29). Joshua's greatness is made known when he and his "household" choose to "serve the Lord" (24:15). Thus, Joshua is the example set before us, and like Joshua we are asked to keep our promises to the covenant.

Many questions and problems surround this text. Is chapter 24 a recounting of the same event that occurred at Shechem in 8:30–35? Or is it a description of an annual ceremony of rededication to the covenant? Scholarship is divided on these questions, but what is clear is that a reaffirmation and renewed dedication to God is described. Making a promise to serve God entails more than just believing. It also means acting on that faith, or putting the promise into action. Like the ancient Israelites, Christians today must "choose this day whom you will serve" (24:15).

CHILDREN'S SERMON ━━━━━━━━━━━━━━

The Truthful Peasant

Once upon a time there lived a king who owned a goat, a lamb, a cow, and a sheep. He loved his animals, so he looked for someone good and kind to care for them. For many years the king had heard tales of a peasant who was known to be a man who never told a lie, had a kind and generous heart, and always kept his word. "He sounds like just the man I want," the king declared. He sent for the peasant and after talking with him gave the peasant the job of caring for his precious animals.

It was agreed upon that every Sunday evening the peasant would visit the palace to report on the animals' health. Every Sunday evening the king would ask, "How is my goat?" and the peasant would answer, "Fine indeed." "And my sheep?" the king would inquire. "Healthy and strong," the peasant would say. "How is my cow then?" the king would ask. "Fit and firm," the peasant would say. "And how is my lamb?" "White and beautiful," the peasant would answer happily.

Things continued to go well for many months. The peasant would report on each animal and then return to his farm in the mountains where he kept the king's animals.

The king was very pleased with his caretaker and often spoke about the man's loyalty. The king spoke so highly of the peasant that one of the king's officials became jealous of the man.

One day, the jealous official said to the king, "Do you really believe this man has never told a lie or broken his promise? I'm willing to bet he has. I'm even willing to bet that he'll tell a lie to you next Sunday."

"I don't believe you," the king said. "And to show you my confidence in the peasant, I am ready to bet my kingdom that he won't lie next Sunday."

The jealous official and the king agreed that whoever lost the bet would lose his position in the court.

Now the official was worried. "How can I make this man lie?" he asked his wife.

"Don't worry, husband," the wife said. "I know how to handle the truthful peasant."

Saturday morning, she dressed in her best clothes and fixed her hair so beautifully that she looked like an angel. She got into her carriage and drove to the mountain farm. When the peasant saw her, he could not believe his eyes. He had never seen anyone so beautiful.

"Good man, will you do me a favor?" she asked the truthful peasant.

"If it is in my power, anything you ask will be done," the peasant answered her.

"I am dying," she said. "The only thing that can cure me is the liver of a healthy lamb. I see you have a fine lamb. Won't you please give me the lamb so I can live?"

"Ask me anything but that," the peasant said. "These are the king's animals. They do not belong to me."

"Oh," the woman began to cry, "couldn't you tell the king that the lamb fell down the mountain and died? If I don't eat a roasted liver, I will die."

"No my lady, I could never lie," the peasant replied.

"I shall die this very night," cried the woman. Then the woman begged and wept, and begged some more. The peasant was touched by the plight of the woman and decided it was best to kill the lamb to save the woman. So he killed the lamb, roasted its liver, and gave it to the woman.

"You have saved me," she said warmly and drove away in her carriage.

Now the poor peasant was horrified. What would he say to the king tomorrow evening? He paced and worried all night long. He tried to rehearse a lie. "Your majesty," he said, bowing low to no one at all. "The lamb has been stol-stol-stol-...," but the lie caught in his throat. He shook his head and tried another. "The lamb has fallen down a mount- mount- mount-...," but again the lie stuck in his throat. No matter how he tried, the peasant just could not tell a lie. "What to do, what to do?" he mumbled as he paced the floor.

The peasant did not sleep that night, but by sunrise he had his answer. So after eating breakfast and feeding the royal animals the peasant grabbed his walking-stick and made the long walk to the palace.

"Good evening, your majesty," he said.

"Good evening, truthful peasant. How is my goat?"

"Fine indeed."

"And my sheep?"

"Healthy and strong."

"And my cow?"

"Fit and firm."

"What is the news of my lamb?"

"My lord and king," the peasant said softly, "I must tell you a story. Yesterday, a beautiful lady came to the mountain. She was quite ill and only I could provide the cure."

He told the story of the dying woman, confessing the death of the lamb.

"Say no more, my good man," the king said. "You were kind enough to cure the dying woman and honest enough to tell me the truth about my lamb."

Everyone in the room cheered and applauded except, of course, the official and his wife. When the king later learned that it was the official and his wife who had tried to trick the peasant, they were exiled from the kingdom.

And as for the peasant? He remained truthful and faithful for the rest of his days.[5]

Reflections on the Story

At first glance this story may seem to be a poor fit. However, on closer inspection this story can enhance our understanding of the Shechem covenant. This text requires a story that contains promise keeping and loyalty. A story for this text should also have the element of consequence(s) for not keeping a promise. Ideally, it should be a story that has three characters: a sovereign, a faithful servant, and an unfaithful servant. "The Truthful Peasant" has these elements. The king and the peasant make a "covenant" agreement concerning the care of the king's property. The king provides for the peasant as long as the peasant takes proper care of the royal property. The king and the court official also are in a "covenant" agreement. As a member of the court it can be assumed that the official has an agreement of some kind with the king. The bet between the two can also be viewed as a "covenant" agreement in its widest definition, as both agree to give up their positions as a condition of the bet.

The central point of the story is not the agreement between these parties but the choice that is made. The peasant must make a choice: to remain loyal to his king or to serve the god of self-preservation. Some may contend the choice is whether to kill the lamb or not, but I contend the killing of the lamb was consistent with keeping his promise to the king. The peasant killed the lamb in order to care for another of the king's "properties": the official's wife. In this selfless act the peasant put into action the covenant agreement, choosing to live out the meaning of the covenant and not the letter of the covenant. The choice of loyalty is in choosing to tell the truth to the king and not choosing the easy way out by lying. The long sleepless night the peasant endured led him to choose that day whom he would serve.

NOTES

[1] J. Maxwell Miller and Gene M. Tucker, *The Book of Joshua* (London: Cambridge University Press, 1974), p. 3; also see Robert G. Boling, *Joshua* (Garden City, New York: Doubleday, 1982), p. 55.

[2] See Genesis 12:2, 13:16, 15:18, 17:2, 17:19, 18:19, 21:13, 22:17, 26:4, 26:28, 32:12, 46:3, 48:4; Exodus 2:24, 6:5, 19:5.

[3] Walter E. Rast, "Joshua" in *Harper's Bible Commentary*, ed. James L. Mays, et al. (San Francisco: HarperSanFrancisco, 1988), p. 236.

[4] Anthony R. Ceresko, *Introduction to the Old Testament: A Liberation Perspective* (Maryknoll, New York: Orbis Books, 1992), p. 84.

[5] An Italian folktale.

Concluding Thoughts

As I said at the outset, teaching and including children in worship is not easy. Yet it is one of the most important activities of the church. We are preparing and laying the foundation for the children's future faith. Storytelling is a means to meet faithfully our obligations to children without dumbing down the gospel message. However, the perfect story for every text does not just magically appear. It must be sought, cultivated, and kept. Which reminds me of a story...

There was once a rabbi who answered every question by telling a story. One day a student asked his teacher, "Rabbi, you can always select just the right story for every question you are asked. What is your secret; how do you do it?"

Smiling, the old teacher replied, "Well, that reminds me of a story. There once was a young soldier who was traveling through the country when he stopped to rest his horse in a small village. As he walked around the small houses he spotted a wood fence. On the fence were nearly forty chalk circles and right in the center of each circle was a bullet hole.

What amazing accuracy, the soldier thought, as he examined the fence. *Not a single shot has missed the bull's-eye.*

The soldier quickly set out to find the person who had such great skill. He was told that the sharpshooter was a small boy.

'Who taught you to shoot so well?' the soldier asked.

'I taught myself,' the young lad replied.

'And to what do you attribute your great skill?' asked the soldier.

'Actually,' the young lad began, 'it's not all that difficult. First I shoot at the fence, and then I take a piece of chalk and draw circles around the holes."

The rabbi chuckled for a moment. "Now you know my secret. I don't look for a story to answer a question. I collect every good story I hear and then store it in my mind. When the right occasion or question arises, I aim the story in its direction. I simply draw a circle around a hole that is already there."[1]

To paraphrase Matthew 13:44, the perfect story is like treasure hidden in a field, which someone found and hid; then in his joy that person goes and sells all that he has and buys the field.

NOTE

[1] A Jewish folktale.

Additional Resources

Barr, David L. *New Testament Story: An Introduction*. Belmont, California: Wadsworth Publishing, 1987.

Barton, Bob, and David Booth. *Stories in the Classroom: Storytelling, Reading Aloud and Roleplaying with Children*. Portsmouth, New Hampshire: Heinemann, 1990.

Bausch, William J. *Storytelling: Imagination and Faith*. Mystic, Connecticut: Twenty-Third Publications, 1991. (Also see other books by Bausch: *Telling Stories, Compelling Stories*, and *Timely Homilies*.)

Bell, Martin. *The Way of the Wolf: The Gospel in New Images*. Phoenix: Phoenix Press, 1984.

Best Loved Stories Told at the National Storytelling Festival (all volumes, by various authors). Jonesborough, Tennessee: National Storytelling Press.

Bettelheim, Bruno. *The Uses of Enchantment: The Meaning and Importance of Fairy Tales*. New York: Alfred A. Knopf Inc., 1976.

Bruchac, Joseph. *Native American Animal Stories*. Golden, Colorado: Fulcrum Publishing, 1992.

Buechner, Frederick. *Peculiar Treasures*. San Francisco: Harper San Francisco, 1989.

Cavanaugh, Brian. *The Sower's Seeds: One Hundred Inspiring Stories for Preaching, Teaching, and Public Speaking*. New York: Paulist Press, 1990.

Cole, Joanna, ed. *Best-Loved Folktales of the World*. New York: Doubleday, 1982.

Courlander, Harold. *The Crest and the Hide: And Other African Stories of Heroes, Chiefs, Bards, Hunters, Sorcerers and Common People*. New York: Coward, McMann & Geoghegan, 1982.

Denman, Gregory A. *Sit Tight, and I'll Swing you a Tail: Using and Writing Stories with Young People*. Portsmouth, New Hampshire: Heinemann, 1991.

Efron, Marshall, and Alfa-Betty Olsen. *Bible Stories You Can't Forget No Matter How Hard You Try*. New York: Dutton, 1976.

Forest, Heather, ed. *Wisdom Tales from Around the World: Fifty Gems of Story and Wisdom from such Diverse Traditions as Sufi, Zen, Taoist, Christian, Jewish, Buddhist, African, and Native American*. Little Rock: August House Publishers, 1996.

Gellman, Marc. *God's Mailbox: More Stories About Stories in the Bible*. New York: Morrow, 1996.

Juengst, Sara Covin. *Sharing Faith with Children: Rethinking the Children's Sermon*. Louisville, Westminster/John Knox Press, 1994.

Livo, Norma J., and Sandra A. Rietz. *Storytelling: Process and Practice*. Littleton, Colorado: Libraries Unlimited, Inc., 1986.

Lowry, Eugene. *How to Preach a Parable*. Nashville: Abingdon Press, 1989.

Mallet, Jerry, and Keith Polette, eds. *World Folktales: A Multicultural Approach to Whole Language; Grades 3–5*. Fort Atkinson, Wisconsin: Alleyside Press, 1993.

Smith, W. Alan. *Children Belong in Worship: A Guide to the Children's Sermon*. St. Louis: CBP Press, 1984.

Walker, Barbara K. *Big Multicultural Tales*. New York: Scholastic Inc., 1993.

Wangerin, Walter. *Miz Lil and Other Chronicles of Grace*. San Francisco: Harper San Francisco, 1988.

_____. *Ragman and Other Cries of Faith*. San Francisco: Harper San Francisco, 1984.

White, William R. *Stories for the Journey: A Sourcebook for Christian Storytellers*. Minneapolis: Augsburg Publishing, 1988.

_____. *Speaking in Stories*. Minneapolis: Augsburg, 1982.

_____. *Stories for Telling*. Minneapolis: Augsburg, 1986.

Williams, Michael E., and Dennis E. Smith, eds. *The Storyteller's Companion to the Bible*. (All volumes in the series, for both the Old Testament and New Testament.) Nashville: Abingdon Press, 1996–.